A Smithsonian Nature Book

HARRIER, Hawk of the Marshes

Frances Hamerstrom

HARRIER

Hawk of the Marshes

The Hawk That Is Ruled by a Mouse

Illustrated by Jonathan Wilde
Photographs by Frederick Hamerstrom
With a foreword by Roger Tory Peterson

Smithsonian Institution Press
Washington, D.C., and London

Published by the
Smithsonian Institution Press,
Washington, D.C.

The paper in this book meets the
guidelines for permanence and
durability of the Committee on
Production Guidelines for Book
Longevity of the Council on Library
Resources.
(∞)

Cover illustration: talon-to-talon
transfer. Painting by Jonathan Wilde.

Library of Congress Cataloging in
Publication Data.

Hamerstrom, Frances, 1907–
Harrier, hawk of the marshes.
Bibliography: p. 144
Summary: Discusses the physical
characteristics and habits of the
Northern harrier as revealed in a
twenty-five year study.
1. [Hawks]
I. Wilde, Jonathan, ill. II. Hamer-
strom, Frederick, ill. III. Title
QL696.F32H35   1986   598'.916
      85-600278
ISBN 0-87474-538-1
ISBN 0-87474-537-3 (pbk.)

Photo credits
Photographs are by Frederick
Hamerstrom except as follows: E. F.
Rivinus, p. 23; William S. Clark,
p. 35; Joe Platt, p. 45; Tom
Meiklejohn, p. 63; Bill Gilbert, p. 66;
Rich Rygh, p. 115; Harry Lumsden,
p. 119.

Dedication

This book is dedicated to Frederick Hamerstrom—without whom my life would have been dulled, and my Harrier Project would never have survived for 25 years—and to the gabboons, who worked longer hours, and harder, than could be expected even of gabboons.

They are listed as they first appeared on the project: Dan Berger, Gary Hampton, Glen Fox, Ray Anderson, Ross Lein, Gary Anweiler, Paul Drake, Chuck Sindelar, Gary Page, Bill Scharf, Tom Ahlers, Joe Platt, Larry Crowley, Ron Sauey, Skip Walker, John Hart, Frank Renn, Dale Griffy, Eric Bienvenu, Brother Edwin Mattingly, Max Albrecht, John Champion, Alan Beske, Deann De La Ronde, Keith Janick, Danny Thompson, Joe Schmutz, Sheila Schmutz, Tina Smith, Keith Bildstein, Curt Griffin, Marc Ashby, Randy Acker, Rodd Friday, Bruce Phillips, Charley Burke, Mark Kopeny, Mac Ehrhardt, Betsy Haug, Dale Gawlik, Dan Groebner, Bill Gilbert, Greg Sulik, Jeff Pope, Rebecca Paulson, Mark Manske, Peter Fasbender, Kevin Turner.

Contents

Foreword

There are two and a half billion women in the world, give or take a few million, but there is only one Frances Hamerstrom.

During the Great Depression of the 1930s, Fran and her adored husband, Frederick, whom she met at a Dartmouth house party, turned their backs on Brahmin Boston and their socialite backgrounds and headed west. Finding their way to the prairies of central Wisconsin, they settled down to the life of pioneers, starting from scratch in the abandoned farmhouse that became their home while they studied prairie chickens.

The saga of the Hamerstroms is told by Fran in her autobiographical book, *Strictly for the Chickens*. Though now older and wiser, she has never lost her youthful taste for adventure nor her offbeat sense of humor. It is evident that both Hamerstroms had inherited the right genes for survival; Frederick is of Viking stock, while Fran claims that pirates were amongst her forebears. Perhaps that explains why she has always had a special passion for the predatory birds.

It was inevitable that Fran Hamerstrom, having spent more than 1,000 mornings with the "chickens," should develop a deepening interest in another resident of the Wisconsin prairies, the northern harrier—or, as it was called until recently, the "marsh hawk." It is essentially the same bird that is known in England as the "hen harrier."

There are 10 species of harriers, all but two in the Old World. They are not true hawks if we are to use that term correctly. In England, which boasts four kinds of harriers, there is one known as the "marsh harrier," which is quite unlike the inappropriately named "hen harrier." To resolve the confusion of names it was decided by the Checklist Committee of the American Ornithologists'

Union to rename our bird the northern harrier. This was a good solution, considering the bird's circumpolar range.

Audubon knew the bird as the "marsh hawk," as did his predecessor, Alexander Wilson, and it must have bred more widely on our continent in their day. Audubon wrote that he had examined nests in the "barrens" of Kentucky and even in Florida and coastal Texas, where these birds now occur only in winter. Today it is nonexistent as a summer resident in the southeastern part of the continent. Only a few pairs persist locally in the New England states, where I live.

On the other hand, vast areas of Canada and Alaska remain suitable for nesting, and therefore the Christmas Bird Counts conducted nationwide by the National Audubon Society do not seem to show any noticeable decline in the numbers of harriers on the wintering grounds.

But in spite of agricultural practices—or perhaps because of them—the prairies and farmlands of the upper midwest remain a stronghold for the graceful harrier. Skimming low over the meadows and marshes, with its wings set in a shallow dihedral, it reminds us somewhat of an owl in its hunting techniques, inasmuch as it seems to depend more on its ears than its eyes to locate its prey.

Dr. Frances Hamerstrom has lectured on bird behavior and ecology in more than a dozen countries. She has authored and co-authored over 75 technical papers and written eight popular books, including *An Eagle to the Sky*. She is the only woman to have received a graduate degree under the late Aldo Leopold. Fran Hamerstrom and her biologist husband have worked as a team for 50 years. Both have received international recognition for their research on birds of prey and prairie chickens. At their home in Wisconsin they now divide their time between the predators and their prey. They are winners of the National Wildlife Federation's Wildlife Conservation Award and have twice won the Wildlife Society Publication Award.

In this new book, Frances Hamerstrom tells us the fascinating story of what she has learned about this slim bird of prey that she has watched and studied for so many years in her beloved Wisconsin.

Roger Tory Peterson

Acknowledgments

Much gratitude for help on the manuscript goes to: Keith Bildstein, William Clark, Mark Fuller, Frederick Hamerstrom, and Ruth Louise Hine. Furthermore, Susi Nehls for some months edited and behaved more or less as though she were my governess to get this manuscript ready for E. F. Rivinus, Senior Science Editor, S.I.P.

Prologue

Mice—I always knew—got preyed on by hawks, and I believed that their populations could be threatened by having too many hawks around. That the hawk, especially if it ate mice, was the farmer's best friend has been an unfounded, but popular belief during the first part of this century, and this belief has not entirely died out yet.

This book traces my voyage of discovery as I gradually learned about the relationship between voles (or meadow mice, as they are sometimes called) and the harrier, a hawk of the marshes. These little mice are the *hawk's* best friend—at least in the case of the harrier. On my 50,000-acre study area, more harriers nest when voles are abundant. Furthermore, when voles are abundant old males tend to indulge in polygyny and take on more mates. And *besides*, when voles are reasonably abundant, and only then, do young males breed—males so young that they are still in immature plumage.

It took me more than 25 years to find these things out and, of all things, to look upon the vole as an aphrodisiac. Actually it took me longer. I could probably call this a 27-year study except that the first two years—1957 and 1958—were almost entirely wasted because I couldn't figure out an efficient way to catch breeding adults.

Appendices at the end of this book contain original data, and dry technical material—not of interest to all.

1 Do Harriers Mate for Life?

April 22, 1957, was still, overcast, and the temperature was close to freezing. I got into my blind and started taking notes before daylight, at 4:15. By 6:38 my morning's field work was done. Two hours and 23 minutes of intense concentration recording prairie chicken behavior lay behind me. My feet were cold and it was time to get out of the blind, drive home in my truck and cook breakfast for a crew of 12.

I was interrupted. At 6:38, 32 Canada geese flew low over the prairie chicken booming ground. I unloaded my mind and watched them wend their way, across rolling grasslands northward past distant birches. Eerie morning light struck the faraway birches white beneath a sluggish leaden sky. For the first time in over two hours I took in the glory of the morning on the marshlands, trying to remember forever the sky and the birches and the sweep of my vast open country.

Frank Fraser-Darling, the great British ecologist who was knighted for his research, admonished us to unload our minds—sometimes to perceive, and sometimes to seize upon a problem or to find a solution. My mind remained unloaded for at least eight more minutes. Instead of wondering if I could get my truck started, and planning to fill the oven with cheese on toast when I got home, I gazed at the birches. My notes read:

"Two harriers are sky-dancing over the marsh. One is almost pure white and the other is slate gray. The white one swings in giant loops like a stunting aviator. The gray one gives a twisting back flip at the top of the loop-the-loop, but he seems to have less style—perhaps because his black-tipped wings are merely gray against the early morning April sky and his dancing loops are smaller—or perhaps it is because he is younger. These dancing males are presumably establishing nesting territories. I wonder about harriers: *do they mate for life?"*

I might have burned the toasted-cheese sandwiches that morning if I had realized that with that question I was launched on a project that was to last 27 years—as irrevocably launched as though a chemical reaction had taken place.

Lady Luck can play a strong part. At the same blind six days later I might have asked a wholly different question. My notes read, "Adult male marsh hawk strikes a juvenile male several times in the air (he's small and brown). The juvenile goes to the ground. The adult stoops repeatedly till the juvenile takes off west—harried about ¼ mile by the adult male. An adult female (large and brown) is nearby during the heckling, but takes no part." In this case the question might well have been, Do harriers fight to establish their breeding territories? In 26 years we have only seen harriers actually hit each other in combat: in 1960 an apparently sick adult male was harassed by a juvenile male. As far as we could determine, we never saw that adult male again. In Idaho, harriers have been seen actually fighting—talon-grappling in the air (16)—but in Central Wisconsin, I would soon have been discouraged if I had asked the wrong question.

Do harriers mate for life? was a lucky question. It looked pretty simple to answer. We had a pair nesting right on our own farm. Catch the male and catch the female and band them. Then catch the pair year after year to see whether or not they remain

mated. It was "our mated pair" that I was after. It was time to build a trap and to study sky-dancing males.

In spring, female harriers all look pretty much alike—largely sparrow-colored, with pale breasts, and the flashy white rump patch that is characteristic of all harriers. But the males vary in plumage. Some appear almost pure white, others are grayish, and the immature males are brown as though to mimic the females. Surely, if I put my mind on it I could memorize the plumage of the sky-dancing male on our 240-acre farm. After all, cattlemen can recognize every one of several hundred different cows at a glance!

At first "our" male seemed medium gray—just dark enough so his black wing tips didn't show up well—but a day or two later I noticed sharp contrast between the gray wings and the black tips of the male sky-dancing over the big marsh on our farm. "Light Gray" had a broken primary on his left wing. The next one I memorized as also "Light Gray," but without a broken primary!

Having read countless bird books, I was convinced that sky-dancing—those marvelous loop-the-loops—was performed by male harriers to advertise their territories and to attract a female. But there seemed to be too many sky-dancing males. Furthermore, I learned to my chagrin that I had failed to develop a knack for recognizing individuals. It was time to get some bands on these birds. But how to catch them?

Starlings: lure birds for harriers.

The bal-chatri is an ingenious trap. It is essentially a cage with a live lure inside. The lure attracts the hawk: dinner! But the hawk will be denied its feast. It has no way to reach into the cage, and furthermore the top of the trap is covered with monofilament nooses. In its attempts to grasp the delectable meal, the hawk "foots" the bal-chatri and before long a toe or two, or even a foot is safely secured and all one needs to do is to disentangle the hawk, pretty up the nooses so they stand upright again in catching position, and anticipate the next catch.

Harriers eat plenty of mice, so mice would seem to be the best lures for attracting these hawks. They're not. After the first few minutes in the cage, mice sit too still; they hide, and they even build nests for better concealment. Such reticence! Birds are better.

Starlings tend to be the best lure birds for harriers. They are restless creatures and continually advertise their presence. Pigeons, on the other hand, are a trifle too large to be attractive to some of the male harriers, and furthermore, their disposition tends to be phlegmatic; they sit about in a bal-chatri as though they had the whole day before them, and nothing else to do. I sometimes circumvent this by sprinkling the inside of the trap with corn. Pigeons, if they have a good appetite, will eat under almost any circumstances . . . happily in a bal-chatri for example. They flutter quite madly just as the hawk is coming in to strike, but once the caught hawk lies still, just a few inches above them, they resume pecking at one of their favorite delicacies: cracked corn.

In the spring of 1957 I built a bal-chatri of poultry wire. (Five years later Dan Berger and I published on this type of trap in the *Journal of Wildlife Management.*) (4) I constructed my first harrier bal-chatri with great care, covered it with 30-pound-test monofilament nooses (the eyes were tied over a knitting needle), and then I set forth to catch starlings for lure birds. We hand-grabbed them in barns at night, as I have described in *Birding with a Purpose,* (30) and soon I had a good enough supply so that every morning I baited my bal-chatri with a starling or two. Then I placed the trap where I hoped a harrier would find it, and crawled into a willow thicket to watch.

On May 12, 1957, I caught an adult male on our farm and banded the first harrier of this study. As I folded his wings against his body, his feathers seemed to have a bloom like the fine dust on a fresh plum. And after folding those big wings, his body seemed almost

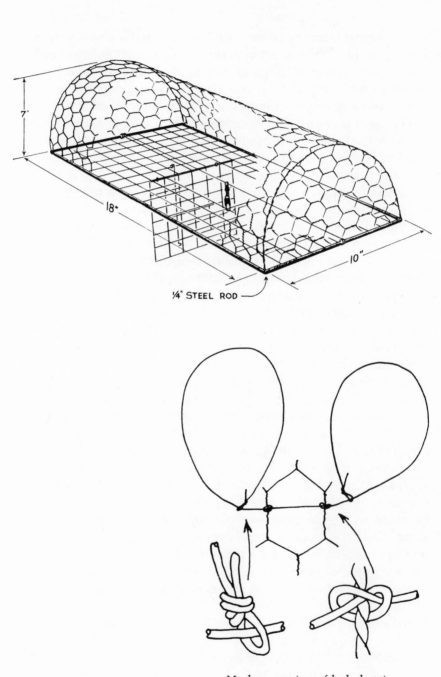

7"

18"

10"

¼" STEEL ROD

Modern version of bal-chatri.

frail. Nine days later I caught a big female. She felt far more rugged. Thereafter, watching the trap became increasingly boring. The joy of bursting out of my hiding place and splashing though the sedges to get my hands on those first harriers began to pale in my memory as the days went by with no more catches. Some mornings—if it was warm enough—I even fell asleep in my hide-away thicket.

In 1958 I caught two migrants, but 1959 was better. Dan Berger, who lived with us and was working on the Prairie Chicken Project of the Wisconsin Conservation Department, finally agreed with me that it was not essential to watch a bal-chatri every moment. We baited eight or ten bal-chatris with pigeons or starlings, jumped into a car to whiz around the fields and marshes dropping off traps, and went back to the house to have naps away from the northwest wind, or the drizzle. Just before lunch, we picked up traps. Starlings and pigeons were returned to our bait room, and we weighed and processed the hawks. We caught 26 harriers on our farm that spring. Would we ever encounter them again?

2   *Major Breakthrough, or the Owl and the Dho-gaza*

Pride goeth before a fall. Elated at having a method for catching harriers, I felt that the little matter of whether or not harriers mated for life was well on its way to being solved. I did have sense enough to realize that information from just one pair nesting on our farm was too small a sample for a pair fidelity study, so I expanded my endeavors to include the 50,000-acre Buena Vista Marsh Prairie Chicken Study Area as well.

Later, in 1959, Gary Hampton, a teen-ager, came to help trap. We decided to run a really big trapline. We both knew that mice were too inconspicuous for summer trapping, so in June we started out each morning with a large cage of bait birds in the back of my VW bus and all the bal-chatris we had on hand. We set the traps out near where we thought there were harrier nests—and we actually found one nest in the process, just by chance.

Trapping in summer was very different from our spring trapping. Heat started to beat down by 10 a.m. almost daily so we worried about the starlings. Pigeons take heat well, but I knew that starlings were better lures: alas, they are delicate in the hot sun. We decided to scatter our traps pretty much over the Buena Vista Marsh—and to change bait, by visiting each trap about every two hours, taking out the tired starling and replacing it with a cool, rested starling from the bait cage in the bus. So now we had to carry *two* bait cages in the bus: one for tired starlings and one for rested ones so we could tell them apart.

Starlings not only do not take heat well, but they like to pry

A starling with a noose around its neck.

with their bills. This lively habit caused a number of starlings to pull nooses through the wire on top of the trap, get hung on a noose, and inadvertently commit suicide. To put a stop to this, we ran a wire along the bottom of the trap to which a small swivel was fastened. Each starling was fastened to the swivel by a collar so it could move to and fro easily along the floor of the trap, but could *not* reach up to seize a noose. We were no longer treated to the depressing sight of starlings dead from hanging.

Nor were we treated to the exhilarating sight of captured hawks. The bal-chatris weren't working because much of the area that we were trapping was meadowland, interspersed with low, sedgy swales and areas of willow and trembling aspen (locally known as popple). As spring moved into summer, the growth of lush vegetation made it increasingly difficult to find bare spots where a harrier could find our traps, and the teeming wealth of songbird reproduction supplied the hawks with plenty of easily caught fledglings, if they wanted a bird diet. We set our traps on sandy mounds thrown up by badgers, on abandoned hay piles, and we knocked down lush vegetation with machetes to fabricate bare spots.

Our lives moved into a pattern: get the traps out by sunup, gulp breakfast out on the marsh, check the traps and replace starlings, run the line, buy gas for the car, gulp lunch, feed starlings, water starlings, keep moving—keep hoping. . . .

One evening after supper, I plunked down in our big red wingchair and announced, "We're not going to put the line out tomorrow."

"Huh?" Gary looked at me as though some previously concealed defect in my character had suddenly emerged. "What *are* you going to do? Quit?"

"I'm going to think."

He turned heel. "And I am going to bed."

Frederick, my husband, and my boss on the Prairie Chicken Project, emerged from his study. "It *is* bedtime, Fran."

"No! Six weeks of this type of effort and not a single hawk caught means that something is very, very wrong."

The house was quiet. Ambrose, my pet great horned owl, flew to the transom over the front door, hoping to be let into the living room to romp—pouncing on pillows and "killing" rubber dolls. This time, for once, I ignored him.

The old house seemed smothered by enormous quiet. The red chair was soft and comfortable, but I was just exhausted by our failure to catch any harriers: I was not sleepy.

A whip-poor-will crashed into his noisy chant close by, and then I listened for his "sub-song." *Whip-poor-will, whip-poor-will* . . . but the sound of the sub-song is muted—like the gentle twanging of low notes on a guitar, and it is uncommon. I felt oddly alert, and was drawn to a bookcase. Christian Ludwig Brehm, 1855, *Vollständige Vogelfang* (11) —*A Complete Compendium of Trapping*— was the book I felt drawn to. I read far into the night—long after the whip-poor-will stopped calling.

I skipped quickly over passages like, "Magpies are sly and harder to catch than crows," or "Blue-throats are caught like nightingales." And then I stopped abruptly and read intently, "Concerning work in the Encyclopédie-Boret, entitled 'The Bird-catcher or secrets ancient and modern of the hunter of birds'. . . . catching a bird of prey with an owl. . . . one often uses an eagle owl to catch birds in nets. . . . the owl should be in motion and trained to fly under the net from perch to perch."

The method of the French bird catcher was plainly being pooh-

poohed, but the author was German, and I knew that most Germans held the French in low esteem in those days. Something like this was worth a try. I spread an old dho-gaza out on the floor to make sure that the net was hung even and flat. Unlike Monsieur, I intended to use *one* net stretched vertically over Ambrose.

Quietly, not to disturb the household, I packed the car for the next morning's venture:

1 dho-gaza

an axe to cut popple (aspen) poles

extra string

binoculars

a perch and leash for Ambrose

bread and peanut butter for the trappers

At last I slipped into bed beside Frederick. He grumbled, "It is very, very late."

I was already wide awake when the alarm went off. After heating up some coffee, I banged on Gary's door.

Gary emerged promptly, looked out of the kitchen window, and exclaimed, "It's still dark!"

"Yes, we need to move fast. Put this leash on Ambrose and tie him somewhere in the car where he'll have a nice perch."

Twists of grass held up the popple poles. Both poles fell when the hawk hit the net.

Gary moved fast. When he got back into the kitchen we downed lukewarm coffee, slipped silently out of the house, and drove toward the big marsh on our farm.

"We need to find where that harrier nest is. Let's get up into some of the oaks along the road to pinpoint it."

Gary selected one oak and I picked another about a quarter of a mile away. (We didn't know then that harriers dislike having people perched in trees in their nesting territory.) We perched for some 40 minutes—from almost deep dark, until direct sunlight set the sedges in the marsh agleam. Almost-white wings of a male harrier flashed high over the marsh, a brown harrier seemed to appear from nowhere; the male dropped the prey he was carrying; the female swept under him and neatly caught it high in the air. She swooped downwind in an arc, and then—after flying low over the sedges— she suddenly side-slipped to the ground near a small clump of willow.

Gary and I slithered down out of our trees and he came running toward me calling, "I've got it! I've got it!" Then he started off toward the nest.

"*Wait*," I shouted, "get the axe out of the car and cut me two straight popple poles about eight feet long."

By the time he returned with the poles I had Ambrose tethered to the block perch. He was about to become a working owl. . . . Gary and I tied the dho-gaza firmly to the popple poles. Gary carried this rig, and I followed with Ambrose and the perch.

We ploshed across the marsh, and just after we passed the willow clump, the female flushed—laboring up out of the sedges. Three small, downy young crouched comfortably on a broad, dry nest of grass and sedge.

I pushed Ambrose's perch deep into the muck. Then Gary and I pushed the butt ends of the popple poles into the muck so that the net between them was flat and taut. The poles wobbled a bit, but I said, "That's just right. They've got to fall when the hawk hits."

My pole was very wobbly, so I wove some sedges to brace its base. The female circled over our heads, cacking during the whole process. Finally we ran back to the car to hide—and to watch. She circled the nest, stooping at Ambrose, but swinging over the net, rather than into it. And then, as though she'd had enough of this nonsense, she flipped around and plunged straight into the net. Both poles broke free and toppled, crossing behind her back so there

He was about to become a working owl.

was no earthly way she could get out. But we rushed in to secure our catch as though every precious moment counted.

Gary started to admire her, but I ordered, "Put her in something and help me set up for the male."

"What'll I put her in?"

For just a moment I examined our vicinity helplessly. Then I said, "Put her in one of your socks." (Before long we were all carrying nylon stockings to store hawks and many other items in.)

Gary had her in one of his socks in a moment or two, and we set up again. I gave Ambrose a swift, soft fingerstroking on top of his

The meadow mouse, Microtus *spp., is a vole. It is about 3.5−5 inches long, has litters of 2 to 9 young—and often has more than one litter a season. It can reproduce very fast—and about every four years its numbers increase dramatically.*

head in appreciation of good work done, and we ran to the car again. We had barely caught our wind when the male appeared. He did no circling, but made one swift, direct stoop into the center of the net and—like the female—was securely caught.

Time to pick up the set and band the birds. Joyously we traipsed back to the car. And it wasn't till we were about to band the female that we noticed that she was already banded! She was one of the 17 females we had caught on our farm!

We had also caught nine males there that spring. I couldn't actually tell which ones had been sky-dancing, but it was plain that most of them had just been passing through on spring migration, and that male harriers not only sky-dance to advertise their territories—*males sky-dance on migration!*

It was also plain that summer trapping near nests was the only way to solve the problem of pair fidelity. Gary reached in his pocket and pulled out a dead meadow mouse which he offered Ambrose. "Here," he said, "I hand-grabbed this for you."

Ambrose took the mouse in his right foot, held it like an ice cream cone, closed his eyes and swallowed it whole. The mouse's short little tail and hind feet went down last.

That voles would soon influence my life and give me an insight on the pair-fidelity problem of harriers never entered my mind at the moment, but it turned out to be the key that unlocked some major mysteries.

Gary said, "Let's get on with the show."

I agreed.

"Let's find another nest to trap."

"No! Let's move fast. We'll go to that nest we've already found."

We dashed off over ten miles of dirt road, set up by the nest (which was in nettles) and caught both the male and the female with dispatch. I looked at my watch: 9:50 a.m. We had caught *two* pairs before ten o'clock in the morning!

This glorious performance was never again to be repeated in the next 24 years.

But it provided, in time, an important first answer to my basic question. Both birds caught at this second nest were recaptured the next year. Each had a new mate.

3 On the Art of Finding Nests

We found harrier nests in the 1930s by one technique. Frederick and I sat on rather far-apart low hillsides in the open country of northwest Iowa. Below us lay a vast marsh. When a brown harrier went back to the exact same spot in the marsh several times, we signalled each other: time to walk in. If one of us had farther to walk than the other he walked fast, so that we would meet at the intersection of our walk-in lines. Presto! we'd find a nest—or if we'd missed the exact spot, all we needed to do was tromp around a bit until we flushed the female.

As the Buena Vista Marsh is flatland I had of course suggested to Gary that we climb trees to get a good overlook; there were no hills. Later we also found other ways of spotting nests—we climbed up to the tops of silos, we perched in windows of abandoned houses, and most often we stood on a cartop carrier.

Since our first find in 1957, we have found 330 nests. These include *centrums*. A centrum is the immediate vicinity of a nest not actually found, but discovered by the presence of flying, still short-tailed young. My aim, starting in 1960, was to find every harrier nest on the whole study area. We undoubtedly missed some nests that failed at egg stage, or when the young were small, but I am convinced that we didn't miss any *successful* nest.

We had apprentices, known as *gabboons*. They came for adventure and to get experience—they got both. Frederick helped me shape them up. We taught each what he most needed to learn: trapping techniques, the scientific method, better public relations, keeping good notes, or acquiring less repulsive table manners.

Most gabboons worked for nothing. We managed to scrounge

money for some who needed it for school, and a few paid us for the privilege of working on the project.

Nest finding was one of the hardest things to teach them. Unlike the open, rolling Iowa country, the Buena Vista Marsh contained areas of 40 to 60 acres of willow, where harriers could hide their nests in small openings. There were popple acreages that were almost as bad. And the big, open meadows were so vast that they could not be scanned with binoculars.

Incubating females have to leave the nest from time to time to preen. Their preen period is about seven o'clock in the morning and lasts about half an hour. They normally sit on a fence post or on a low bush. Any female harrier seen sitting about, at the time of day that most people are eating breakfast, is worth watching and following with complete concentration. She may hunt for a while, she may feed, she may sit and scratch her head, or she may take off and disappear behind a bush, but if you are reasonably lucky she will lead you to her nest.

I taught the gabboons this method of finding nests, and also the classic method: watch the male drop food to the female; she will return to the nest. But we found we had a great deal more to learn before we became really adept at nest finding. In the first place, the female doesn't always return straight to the nest—not by any means! She may take the food down to a favorite plucking spot and eat part of it herself. And after that she may take it to another spot—possibly to eat a little more. These little visits to favorite spots do not show one where the nest is. But in time we found that females spend less than ten minutes at these favorite spots, and that when a female has remained down for ten minutes she is, at last, on the nest.

We also learned that if a female suddenly side-slips or parachutes into the vegetation, rather than flying in to land, she has side-slipped onto a nest.

And the nest, not infrequently, is just behind a clump of willow or in some low spot, so if you are alone, and have a line on it, but no good marker to let you know how far to walk the line, the rule is "Keep walking; it's almost always farther than you think." (A mile and a quarter is the longest line I have ever walked, and I was dead-on and flushed her.)

Lines must be walked very exactly. Every time one gets a line on a nest, one makes a map before taking a single step. One must

28

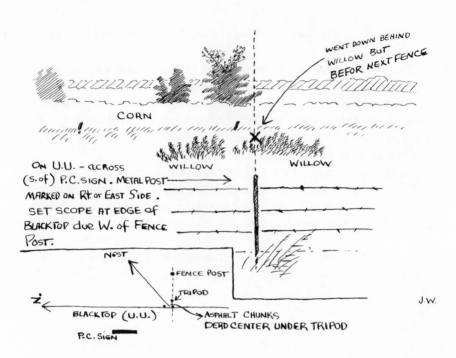

Copy of a gabboon sketch, marking the nest site.

be careful to include a distinctive feature high on the far horizon.

The map had better be good. It always looks like a sure thing, but every map made by a gabboon is supposed to be so good, that somebody else can walk that line. And, as we try to wait until the eggs have hatched, the next walk-in may be some weeks later. Frank Renn, I believe, once made such a good map that I walked his line for a quarter of a mile. I was barefoot, and suddenly my foot touched one of the eggs in the nest!

People walking a line look like pictures of sleep-walkers; their heads are held high and their eyes are on one small object, like the barely distinguishable tip of a far-distant white pine. Walking a line to a nest requires enormous concentration and often considerable ingenuity as well. There are badger holes to fall into. After a tumble, that precious, tiny landmark on the far horizon is not easy to identify.

"Back-track," I tell the gabboons. "Just 20 yards or so of back-tracking will give you your precise direction so you can pick up the landmark on your map." They nod their heads, and some learn to utilize back-tracking. Others seem to find these instructions so obvious that they look at me as though I were stupid.

A far more difficult problem is having to cross a drainage ditch or a creek. Your distant landmark disappears as you go down, so you must memorize a tuft of grass or a weed that lines up with it; wade through the water (sometimes chest-deep); and before you reach that little old weed it is time to find your distant landmark again.

So much for finding nests in relatively simple terrain. Finding nests buried in some small opening in head-high thickets is a real challenge, and so is a long walk-in with ups and downs in the terrain. It takes two gabboons to handle these efficiently. One climbs up onto something high at the beginning of the walk-in, armed with a scope so he can keep track of the walker's whereabouts, and a flag on a long pole so he can signal him. The other carries a fairly long pole topped with a flag so he can be seen, and binoculars so he can see the signals.

The signals are simple: flag to the right—move right; to the left—move left; flag straight up—you're right on the line. There is one more signal: flag down and flagman lying down. This means he is signalling, "I wish I were dead; you are doing the wrong thing."

"The wrong thing" almost always means "The nest is still farther. Don't come back!"

An experienced flagman lets the walker go well *beyond* the nest if the female doesn't flush. It is far easier to steer someone *toward* you if he is facing you, rather than having him turn around to look at you from time to time.

People walking a line look like pictures of sleep-walkers.

A flagman's signals to a walker. The third photo means, "I wish I were dead; you are doing the wrong thing."

The distances in open country are sometimes so great that the walker has to *keep* using binoculars not to lose his faraway landmark: his arms get tired.

I have tried two approaches to working in head-high cover with no one to help me. Early one morning in late July I got two lines on a nest, roughly at right angles. Using a compass, I first walked one line. I overshot, and missed the nest. The dew was so heavy that my path left an easily visible trail through the willows. I rushed back to the car, and then—again using the compass—I walked the other, glancing to right and left to pick up the intersection with my earlier dew trail. It worked. I found the intersection near an obvious opening about 10 yards away and flushed the female in a very few minutes. The nest, a late one, contained two eggs!

I used another approach in what looked like a hopeless thicket. I got a line on the nest by perching in a tall cottonwood. Instead of choosing a landmark on the horizon, I counted telephone poles along a road beyond the thicket, and planned just where to park my car. In a leisurely manner I climbed down out of my tree, parked the car at that exact spot, and stuck a kitchen match under the horn button so the horn would keep blowing. Then I ran back to my tree and proceeded to follow the sound. This idea seemed brilliant to me, but one of my ears hears better than the other so I have trouble locating sounds with precision. The outcome of this endeavor was that I never found the nest, but I did succeed in running down the car's battery.

The record for nest finding, as far as I know, is held by Hammond and Henry. (32) By purposefully poking around in a canoe on the Lower Souris Wildlife Refuge in North Dakota, I'm told they found seven nests in one day! In Wisconsin, harrier nests have been found on muskrat houses in emergent vegetation.

On the island of Orkney, north of Scotland, where Eddie Balfour did his sterling research on the rather closely related hen harrier, I saw still another style of nest hunting. The gently rolling hills are covered with heather; there are lush marshes in the lowlands where I thought harriers should nest. But the Orkney harriers ignored the lush marshes and nested high in the hills, selecting small sedgy pockets! Balfour could find his nests with comparative ease by glassing from a nearby hill, or by looking up into the hills from the lowlands.

There are three different species of harriers in Britain. According to Hollom, (36) the Montagu's harrier tends to nest in rank marsh vegetation, also on heaths with gorse bushes, bramble thickets, etc., as cover. The marsh harrier nests among reeds and rank vegetation growing in water. The hen harrier usually nests in a hollow on the ground.

The Northern harrier, our North American bird, is actually the same species as the hen harrier, but a different race. The nesting of some European species is charmingly described by Henning Weis in *Life of the Harrier in Denmark: Observations from Breeding Places in West Jutland.* (48) Instead of being limited in its nest-site selection like the European birds, as far as I know our harrier has taken over all their niches with the exception of heaths. I have been told that harriers have nested in the Rocky Mountains in sagebrush—at altitudes of over 5,000 feet; and on the island of Martha's Vineyard, off the Massachusetts coast, they nest in expanses of old, but only knee-high, oak trees.

It came as a surprise to many when Donald Watson found the British hen harrier nesting in "forests." Dr. K. W. Brewster pointed out to me that the nests, to be sure, were within plantations, but in openings created by rocky outcrops, etc. rather than in the forest proper. Watson's concept of a forest and the North American concept of a forest are so different that it is hard for me to grasp what his "forest" nest sites might look like. Watson did say, (45) "The height of the surrounding conifers varied greatly, from about 1.50 metres to over six metres. The harriers showed a marked preference for the more open parts of the forest. . . . All forest nests were in plantations at least five years old." These descriptions do not bring up visions of a North American forest.

The British call streetcars "trams," baby buggies "prams," and even five-year-old plantations seem to rate as a "forest." It is a difference in terminology, rather than a difference in physiography. We have seen some of the Scottish plantations. Fraser-Darling pointed them out to us with pride. Aesthetically, they are squared-off, monotype blocks of planted conifers, breaking the wide sweeps of open country that constitute the famous grouse moors; politically they are encouraged by the Forest Commission—but perhaps I should limit my discussion to the effect of plantations on the hen harrier.

I have a theory as to why Watson's birds were drawn to plantations in the first place. Furrows are made by tree-planting machines when new plantations are established. Furrows break up the existing vegetation, and this tends to produce excellent habitat for voles. An abundance of voles (as I will show later) attracts nesting harriers. I believe Watson's hen harriers were attracted by the voles in the new plantations, and that they persisted in trying to nest in the same area. Watson's birds in the conifer plantations may well have been successful parents that kept returning to the same nesting area, even though it was becoming more and more unsuitable.

I know an alder swamp in Rusk County, Wisconsin, where a pair of harriers nested deep in the tall alders. How long ago was that alder swamp an open marsh—optimum harrier nesting habitat?

With wetlands being drained, harriers are losing optimum habitat in many areas. They are also losing nesting areas because of fire suppression; their marshes are growing up into thickets.

In trying to preserve harrier habitat we must not forget that many harriers—as well as other species—are often not nesting in the best places. The all-powerful force of plant succession has forced many species to hang on—temporarily—in second-rate range. Under natural conditions fire, flood, and sometimes beaver dams set back marshland successions so that marshes were renewed.

Modern man—in order to protect property—normally prefers to ignore the value of fire, prevent floods, and get rid of beaver.

4 *Identification of Harriers*

Field Identification: The harrier is a convenient species to work
on in North America: the adult males are easily identified by their
grayish plumage, the females and juveniles are brownish, the males
are smaller than the females, and all harriers have white rump
patches. Furthermore, if you see two brown harriers flying near
each other and one is noticeably smaller—it's a male.

If you can sneak close enough to a perched brown harrier to get
a good look at its eyes, and if the eyes are chocolate, the bird is a
female and not yet a full adult. If the eye of this brown bird is grayish brown or straw colored, it is a young male.

Next we come to the fine points: juvenile harriers have no
molt until the next summer (when they are a year old). They have
deep rufous tawny breasts and very dark backs and wings from the
time they leave the nest and are free-flying, so it is easy to distinguish birds of the year from older females. (Obviously it is easy to
distinguish between them and the old gray males.) But juvenile harriers have lost their Rhode Island Red-colored breasts by spring!
The breast feathers have faded to almost white, and it is no longer
possible to tell them from adult females by plumage—except for
one little trick which Bill Clark, an expert on hawks, told me. A
dark patch under the wings characterizes the immatures.

And now we come to still finer points: before mid-June, in the
Lake States, and probably throughout the breeding range, any har-
rier with gaps in both wings at about Primaries Number 1 through
Number 3 (roughly near the center of the wing) is an adult female.

These gaps are present because the adult females have dropped feathers and have started molting. The yearlings and the males will commence their molt later in the season.

Not a few bird watchers become suspicious of you if you watch a hawk—obviously a harrier—winging its way far above you against the bright blue spring sky and they hear you exclaim, "There goes an adult female." My suggestion is to get them to place a bet with you. Then refer them to the extraordinary work of two harrier gabboons, Josef and Sheila Schmutz, who published on the relationship between molt and nest-brood events in the *Auk*. (42) (The gaps must occur symetrically in both wings and in just the right position. There is still some illegal hawk shooting going on. Even though gunners can make gaps in wings by mising the body of their target, not even a rifle can eliminate Primaries Numbers 1 through 3 on both wings without killing the hawk.)

Anyone who has struggled with field identification of the only species of harrier in North America can sympathize with the problems of the European bird watchers, who might see three of their four species in one day—and the females and juveniles of at least two species are said to look very much alike! This caused enormous confusion in earlier times. In Britain there are three species,

A dark patch under the wings characterizes the immatures.

36

the males of all three of which were correctly named, but ornithologists thought that the females were still another species,
which they called "Ringtails" because of their barred tails! Even
now in Britain, female harriers are affectionately called ringtails. I
was taught in New England to call *raccoons* "ringtails"—a nice
woodsy name for these sizeable mammals. It is a bit unnerving to
go birding in Britain and have an authority point high in the sky
and joyously shout, "Ringtail!" The harrier plate in Peterson,
Montfort, and Hollom's *A Field Guide to the Birds of Britain and
Europe* (39) is useful in telling adult harriers apart, although it
scarcely shows the juveniles. And Donald Watson has an excellent
popular discussion in his book, *The Hen Harrier.* (45) Having just
one species of harrier in North America has simplified my life
immeasurably.

Identification of Nestlings: Small, downy hawklets of all species
all look pretty much alike to me. For harriers my method of identification is simple. If the nest is on the ground and parent harriers
are screaming at me when I visit it—it is a harrier nest.

Sexing of nestlings is slightly more complicated: female downies already have thicker tarsi than the males even when they are
very small. But every now and then a slightly abnormal downy will
be impossible to sex: is it a thick-ankled male or a slender-ankled
female? Abnormality in thickness of tarsi is not frequent. Adult
males normally take a U.S. Fish and Wildlife Service Number 4
band and adult females a Number 5. Of 301 birds that we banded,
only two males required a Number 5 and only one female required
a Number 6.

In 1963, I noticed that nestling males have grayish brown irises,
whereas those of the nesting females are chocolate. These differ-
ences are clearly detectable after the downies are 11 days old. Even
novices have no trouble in detecting the difference in color if the
nest contains young of both sexes, but they do tend to become dis-
traught if the nest contains five young of the same sex because they
can't see the difference in color.

Identification with Bird in Hand: Males and females are easily
separated by weight and wing measurement.

The weighing of a high-energy, nervous bird like a wild hawk
can be accomplished with utter simplicity. Put the hawk into a

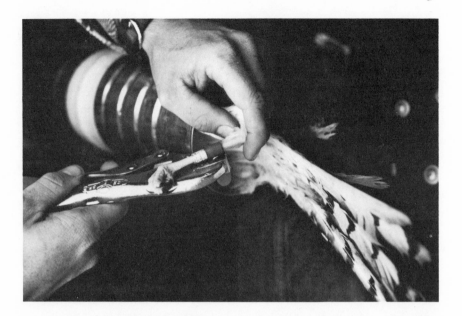

Harrier in tube ready for weighing.

Toes hold the tip firmly so the wing can be stretched and flattened for measuring.

long tube made of fruit juice cans—two 4½-inch-diameter cans for females, one 3¼-inch can for males. One end has small breathing holes, the other is wide open so the bird can void, passing its splashy whitewash (urates) easily whenever it wants to. Hawks not infrequently seem to fall asleep within the cool, dark tube. I suspect that they really do. On the other hand, as I have pointed out in *Birding with a Purpose*, (30) owls tend to struggle violently in the dark, so we weigh them in the light, confined in nylon stockings.

Every now and then when we are weighing a harrier—and we tend to take them to the car, where the rather heavy scales are kept—we hear the sound of brakes and somebody stops to see what we are up to. Nowadays the world contains numerous busybodies who threaten to report us for stuffing a live hawk into a tube!

I ask gently, "Do you know how to keep a hawk happy while it is being weighed?" Then I tell them about the hawks in the tubes and about the owls in nylon stockings. If they are still hostile, I ask them what they would do if they encountered a hawk with a broken wing. "Would you put it in a nice, big parrot cage to take it to a veterinarian?" Members of the public tend to nod.

"That," I admonish them sternly, "is about the most cruel thing you can do. Can't you see that the poor bird will keep struggling? And bash itself against the walls of the cage until its wrists and cere (that tender, soft part of its beak) are all bloodied? Can't you see that it is kinder to transport a hawk in a cool, dark tube?"

Weighing a hawk is really rather simple, but coping with busybodies is not.

An (to me) astonishing number of museum skins of harriers are mislabeled.

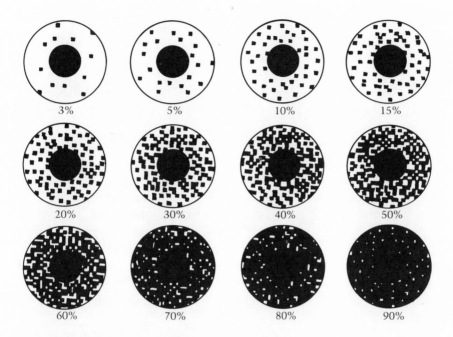

3%   5%   10%   15%

20%   30%   40%   50%

60%   70%   80%   90%

Proportions of eye spotting in iris of female harrier. Percentage (%) of flecking (dark) decreases with age.

Measuring wings needs to be done with care. The bird's body must be held high enough, and near the ruler, so that the shape of the chord is not distorted. The Europeans measure the flattened wing, being careful to get the full length from bend to tip. For comparison of chord versus flattened-wing measurements and weights of the American harrier in Wisconsin and the hen harrier in Scotland, see the Appendix.

We measure both the flattened wing and the chord, in part because I want to compare my measurements with those of the Europeans. But I have a more devious reason. If one of the gabboons brings in figures with an improbable discrepancy between these two measurements from the same bird, it behooves me to take him to task, and to have him practice measuring in front of me so I can figure out what he is doing.

The common mistake in museum specimens is that brown male harriers are labelled "adult female"—and these mistakes have crept into the literature. It took a bit of sleuthing to find out how these mistakes (mostly in the older specimens) kept occurring. I have unearthed two reasons: Before the turn of the century, most museums only wanted birds in full breeding plumage, and until recently it was not known that brown subadult males rather frequently breed. The other reason came as something of a shock to me: museums paid more for breeding *adults*, so if a dishonorable collector labelled a brown male "Adult female," he would get more money!

In North America female harriers can be aged to the year with a fair degree of certainty by eye color until they are five years old. The chocolate irises of the subadults tend to turn amber in the second year. Gradually the percentage of brown flecks decreases at a fairly constant rate (although there is some individual variation). (24) Almost all females known to be over five years old have yellow irises—pale yellow like the yolks of hen eggs bought in an American supermarket. Curiously, the female irises of the closely related hen harrier have an orange tinge—more like that of the yolks of hens that have roamed around free to eat what they please in a farmyard.

Females, by the way, are not old when they are five-year-olds. A harrier was known to live 16 years and 5 months in the wild. (14)

Adult male harriers have bright lemon-colored eyes. The grayish brown eyes of the young turn to pale straw during the first winter of life. Males also have slimmer tarsi.

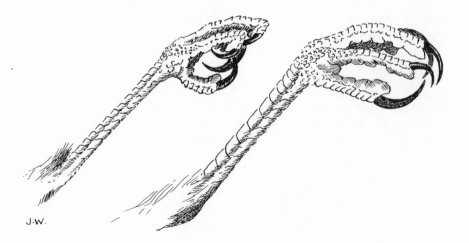

J·W.

Sexing by tarsi: The female's is thicker.

Fault bars on primary.

Ageing by Fault Bars: When birds undergo great stress at the time that they are growing one or more new feathers, the growing feather is weakened, and this weakness leaves a mark on the feather. Fault bars are particularly common in meat-eating birds. We used to call these bars "hunger streaks," but now suspect that severe stresses other than hunger may also produce them—perhaps cold; and certainly fault bars can result from injury to the base of a growing feather.

The fault-bar technique for ageing is particularly useful for birds like those owls that have plumage that looks the same for both immatures and adults. For harriers I have only had to resort to it for females found dead in spring. Their breast feathers were bleached almost white like an adult's and they had been dead long enough so that I couldn't tell whether their eyes had been chocolate or yellow at the time of death.

The method is rather like detective work, but actually simple. It is a matter of asking oneself the right questions:

At what age do birds grow all their wing and tail feathers at once? *Only* when they are nestlings.

At what age do birds grow just two or three feathers simultaneously on both wings? *Only* when they are a year or more old.

Understanding the sequence in which harriers molted their feathers used to strike me as peculiarly worthless information— that is, until it came time to mark birds for individual recognition.*

---

*For further information on molt see the Appendix.

5   *We Resort to Paint, Dyes, and Jesses*

Back in 1960 I had trouble identifying the male at one of the nests in the south end of the study area. I caught him, banded him, and considered cutting the tips of a couple of wing feathers so I could recognize him again. He was molting and I didn't know which feathers he was going to drop next so clipping at random seemed a poor solution. I was reluctant to let that bird go without some distinctive mark to set him apart from the others, so I just sat in the car, harrier held in hand, and pondered. I put him in a tube and started rummaging around in the back of the car where I might find something useful. Under a bag of tools and the shovel lay one can of green spray paint—left over from marking snowy owls. The container still had the right sound when I shook it to mix the paint, and in a matter of moments I sprayed the harrier's left wing and the left half of his tail bright green. The green underwing showed up beautifully upon take-off, but harriers—normally low-flying—tend to show their uppersides, and the uppersides of both sexes are so dark that even a thorough paint job would not show to advantage. However, "Green Left" was about to teach me a great deal.

Green Left—apparently untroubled by his flashy plumage—reared young successfully, and *early* the following summer I managed to catch him again. First, I read his band number, and then I looked for traces of green paint. It didn't take a hand lens to see last year's paint on some feathers and not on others. I knew exactly which feathers were left over from last year and which had been replaced!

It was through Green Left that we developed a technique, less messy than painting, that we called *punching*. We needed to make a small mark for recognition on the flight feathers of birds we were apt to catch again. At first we made these marks with a conductor's punch, but later we found we could make them more simply with scissors.

Fault bars are sometimes so severe that part of the vane of the feather drops off. We made our little cuts at a different slant to avoid possible confusion, and we punched only the right side or the left so we'd have virgin territory the following year for our molt records.

Punching was the first step in being sure we understood the progression of the molt. Harriers, unlike falcons, molt their primaries in an orderly manner, starting with Number 1 near the middle of the wing and proceeding toward Number 10, the farthest from the body. By 1961 we were ready for a far more sophisticated marking technique: *imping*.

Imping is an ancient falconers' technique. The word is derived from the Latin verb *imponere*, to place within. Treasured hawks, flown by falconers, sometimes broke or damaged feathers and these were carefully repaired by replacing the damaged part of the feather with another feather.

Falconers take great care to strive for a perfect match and the new addition can scarcely be detected. Our imps were made with exactly the opposite viewpoint! We wanted the imped feathers to show. And now the information gained from Green Left, and from punching became extremely useful. We imped brightly colored feathers, and we selected the two newest feathers in the hawk's wing to receive our gaudy imps. We figured that two adjacent, brightly colored feathers would show up better than one.

Furthermore, we wanted our imps long enough for good visibility, so instead of using an imping needle, we cut off the bird's

J.W.

Punch mark near tip of feather, not easily confused with fault bar.

Top is a falconer's imp and bottom are colored feathers ready to put into a harrier wing.

own new feather about a half inch from the skin of the wing. This left a substantial hollow shaft. (Those who have plucked chickens will recall that the base of most feathers is hollow and tends to be somewhat translucent.)

We glued the butts of our brightly colored imps into the hollow shaft with Duco household cement, made sure that the imps weren't twisted and were lined up with the bird's own feathers, held the bird for three or four minutes, and released it.

I started building up a collection of suitable white feathers to dye for imping. Feathers of white chickens were easily obtained, but the curve in the flight feathers of members of the chicken family is far too strong to lie well next to the relatively straight feathers of a hawk's wing. For male harriers the feathers of pigeons are

Holding an imped harrier ready to go.

satisfactory; for females I usually had to resort to wing feathers of small white ducks, or of gulls.*

A neighbor raised White Kings so primaries of big pigeons were no problem; a few of my friends went beachcombing and sent bundles of tattered gull feathers. At last I telephoned a commercial duck producer: Yes, I could have all the feathers I wanted—he'd be slaughtering in a week. I drove 60 miles to the duck producer; there were barrels of feathers—and not a single primary was hard-penned! A hard-penned feather has a smooth pointed base—just right for imping—and one that is not hard-penned, but still growing, with blood in the quill, breaks awkwardly, and lacks the smooth point needed for imping. (No wonder that roast duckling tends to be so tender: the ducklings are butchered before their feathers are fully grown out.) Reluctantly I left my duck producer, drove home, and painstakingly gathered duck feathers from local farmyards.

We always had to make sure that the harrier feathers we selected to receive the colored imps were also hard-penned or they would fall out within the hour. I colored my white feathers with Rit or Diamond dyes, boiling buckets of feathers in the kitchen. The colors faded during the winter, but in spring, when the harriers returned from migration, I could still identify last year's birds.

The adult males normally get back to the breeding grounds first, and the adult females (followed by the subadults) return later. One spring the very first harrier was a female. I watched from a bridge; she was big and brown and each time she swung low over the pussy willows I could read her imps: she was Pink Left. _Pink!_ I had never dyed a feather pink! She quartered a meadow, coming nearer and nearer until I could spot her imped wing without binoculars. Pink—and then I remembered standing on the same bridge last year and watching Red Left quartering past her nest and toward me. So Red had faded to Pink.

Theoretically my imps should stay in 11 months. They should stay in until they are molted with the feather shafts they were glued into. So theoretically I should be able to spot my breeders when they return from their wintering grounds in the South. But

---

* To give an idea of how restrictive our laws are getting, I might mention that a federal permit is needed to pick up even a gull feather from the beach!

The plastic jesses are bright colored.

this was the first time that it had actually happened: Red Left was in position by her last-summer's nest. Now to watch for her mate.

Weeks later we found two nests a mile apart near the bridge. One had a male imped Green-Green, whose mate was unbanded, but the second nest had a banded female! Who was she? This exasperating female was aggressive, dive-bombed Ambrose—my decoy owl—with vigor, but missed the net every time. And each time this reaction wore off she *distress-circled* high above her nest, as though to call in help. And help came. A flashy, unbanded male zoomed in to dive-bomb Ambrose; and—to my intense surprise— Green-Green appeared and stooped close to the net, but we still failed to catch that banded female.

We climbed her favorite perch trees and fastened noose carpets on the tiptops: she perched elsewhere. We tried using a very wild snowy owl, who had a tumor on her wing and tried to bite people; she fought me all the way across the marsh. I got bitten and footed, but she failed to entice our banded female into the net. (That snowy owl is the only raptor I've encountered who persistently attacked people and was untameable. After nursing her for months, our veterinarian declared her tumor inoperable and she was stuffed for a school museum shortly after I had tried out her talents on our banded female.)

Bird books say that hawks do not make kills near their nests, and I had believed this, so it was as a last resort that we put a balchatri, baited with a pigeon, a few yards from her nest. We had spent about two weeks studying that bird's behavior—primarily in order to catch her. We learned that distress-circling by a female suggests that there is a nest below; we learned that only one male—the flashy, unbanded one—brought food and regularly defended this nest; and we learned that harriers may try to make kills close to the nest. She tried for the pigeon and got caught.

Now, by mid-summer, she was no longer wearing imps; they had molted, so it was not until I finally had her in my hand and read her band number that I knew who she was. It was dizzying. She was Pink Left of early spring; she had been mated to Green-Green last year. She was fickle: her last-year's mate was alive and nesting just a mile away. My pair-fidelity study was about to become complex.

Of course it was worth two weeks to document a case of infidelity but spending ten days to catch one hawk is scarcely strategic effort. We needed permanent markers. We discovered stout light-weight plastic strips, originally designed for durable webbing on outdoor furniture. These came in half-inch widths and big rolls. Jesses made of this material were better than colored bands because they projected about three-fourths of an inch and gave better visibility. This magnificent material lasts at least seven years and the colors do not fade. Wildco Instruments, Saginaw, Michigan, produced it for a while, but they are discontinuing this product, and as far as I have been able to determine, both good lawn-chair webbing and Grade A marking material for hawks are no longer on the market.

I hoard my meagre supply.

6   *On the Care and Feeding of Gabboons*

The Harrier Project has always been confronted by challenges.
Even the relatively simple matter of how to apply plastic jesses was
a problem. At least we had both hands free, as jesses can be put on
when the hawk is resting in a tube. First we tried knotting the jesses,
but stiff plastic makes for plump knots, and we feared that the females might not be able to incubate properly with lumpy knots on
their tarsi. Next we turned to Speedy Rivets. Each half of a Speedy
rivet will fit nicely into a little hole punched into the plastic, and
all it takes to make the jess secure is a solid substrate and a sharp
blow with a hammer. I put the leg of the tubed hawk up close to a
brick, get the rivet in position, and give a sharp blow with a hammer. It sounds easy. But the sharp blow from the hammer must hit
the rivet dead-center—and dead-center is unnervingly close to the
leg of the harrier. I never missed once, but always dreaded the moment of the sharp blow.

Teaching the gabboons the art of the sharp blow was another
matter. All of the gabboons had a deep love for birds of prey, and
many of them were falconers and felt personally involved with each
hawk they handled. One day Frederick appeared and overheard a
typical conversation.

"Look," I ordered in exasperation, "you can't just give that rivet
little taps. You've got to whang it home."

"I'm afraid I'll break the bird's leg."

"Well, you'd better not."

"Fran, I wish *you'd* do this."

"If you're ever going to amount to anything, you'll do it." By now I was shouting. "You won't have me around as a nursemaid for the rest of your life."

Frederick gave a little cough. He does not like shouting.

The gabboon, his hairy chest glistening with effort, crouched hammer in hand, and cast Frederick an imploring look.

Frederick's voice is always quiet. "Just a moment. I have an idea." Frederick rummaged in the tool box, found a pair of vise-grip pliers, adjusted them, and snapped the rivet shut. Vise-grip pliers became standard equipment.

With a 50,000-acre study area to cover, we worked in pairs only at the very beginning of the season: one as a teacher and the other as a pupil. Everyone was supposed to be able to do everything, and to work alone most of the time. One exception was Tom Ahlers. He was already on the project before I discovered that he was color-blind. So various children, bird watchers, and novices had to accompany him in the field to read colors of jesses and imps.

Imping a hawk without a helper is moderately complicated because, unlike jessing, it cannot be done with the bird in a tube. The system is to sit, or kneel on the ground and hold the hawk's legs firmly between one's knees, as in a gentle vise. This leaves both hands free for imping the wings. I gave the new gabboons a demonstration. The next day John Hart successfully trapped a female harrier. He weighed her, measured her, jessed her, and then he brought her into headquarters saying, "I don't know how to imp her. I can't hold her."

"Of course you can. She won't hurt you if you hold her firmly between your knees."

I was pretty disgusted that anyone as muscular and capable-looking as John would mind the slight danger of getting footed by a hawk that weighed little more than a pound.

John tried to tell me something, but I interrupted, saying, "Here's Frank, he'll show you."

Frank, a Senior Gabboon, has a real knack for getting other people to do things. I went into the kitchen to cook lunch. After I got the mulligan simmering and plopped a bread pudding in the oven, Joe Platt called, "Frank needs your help."

Frank seldom needed help so I went back into the study with dispatch. All the gabboons (we had four that summer) demonstrated a mien of disrespectful anticipation. Were they ganging up on me?

Frank waved a languid hand toward John. "You try, Fran."

I pulled the hawk out of the tube and handed her to John. "O.K., you're holding the feet right, now put your knees together." John tried. His mighty thigh muscles kept his knees about three inches apart.

"Kneel down on the floor and try it," I said in a very different tone.

Four gabboons hooted in delight at my discomfiture.

The selection of a crew for field research is always fraught with problems. From now on I had to size up potential gabboons not only for stamina, dedication, and a knack for handling hawks; but also as to color vision and the anatomy of their legs.

Gabboons need to be watched. One of the most important things that they need to be taught is caution. For example, "Fran, the same bird was there again today."

Gently, I inquire, "How do you know?"

"It was sitting on the same fence post."

"Look," I have to point out, "recognizing the same bird that way is not a sure thing. You wouldn't recognize people by which chairs they sat on, would you?"

Another type of caution is also necessary. Throughout the years only two gabboons have had to be hospitalized. Keith Janick ran up a fever that stayed near 104°, but he got well in a few days. Then Larry Crowley rolled Frederick's car on a curve, but was well enough in a week or two to trap harriers on crutches.

We lent the gabboons our cars, and due to the multitude of accidents, we finally didn't dare collect insurance—lest our rates go up. We just paid the bills. Some summers this cost more than *feeding* the crew.

Gabboons, almost without exception, have magnificent appetites—and some have a taste for expensive delicacies. It has been my policy to hide these. This works well enough with cakes and pies, but it's hard to hide ice cream anywhere other than the freezer. We rationed ice cream.

Feeding a crew well is important. It keeps the morale up. The cook in a lumber camp is said to have a good deal of power. I, the Harrier Project leader, confess that I sometimes baked pies as rewards for accomplishing difficult missions.

7 How We Learn from Marked Birds

In 1961 we imped Male Yellow-Green. He defended the nest with vigor and was easy to catch. Then we went to a nest less than a mile away hoping to catch another pair. Yellow-Green defended this nest too, and he brought food to the female! Bigamy! Yellow-Green plainly had two mates! His interest in these two nests was not the casual interest of the subadult male whom Pink Left had attracted when she went distress-circling, nor the casual interest of her mate of the year before who had dive-bombed Ambrose a few times. This male assiduously tended both females and we were dealing with imped, easily recognized individuals.

Robert Hecht in 1951 reported bigamy in harriers at Delta, Manitoba. (34) At that time only two cases of bigamy in harriers had been reported in the literature. Hecht watched a male tending two nests. Hecht's major professor doubted his findings and I tended to doubt them too. It was direct observation on a wide-open marsh. I no longer doubt Hecht's pioneer findings even though his birds were unmarked.

It was tempting to settle down to a study of Yellow-Green's behavior toward his two mates, but we had to move on and trap at other nests. I couldn't let one "aberrant" male interfere with my whole pair-fidelity study. I carried Ambrose over to a nest about half a mile from Yellow-Green's second nest and took a gabboon along so we could set up quickly. Dale shoved the owl perch into the ground, I fastened Ambrose's leash quickly, and just as it was time to set the dho-gaza poles Dale exclaimed, "Fran—"

"Hurry," I interrupted, "listen how she's cacking! Hurry!"

"But Fran—"

"Will you get your end of the net up?"

Dale just pointed at the sky, where a male circled and cacked. He shouted so I would get the message. "It's Yellow-Green! He just brought her food!"

Yellow-Green defended three nests and brought food to three females—*a trigamist*!

Now, many years later, I realize that Yellow-Green was a remarkable male—not because he had three mates, but because he helped all three females bring off their broods successfully. Even when a male has only two mates, the nest of the less-favorite spouse is apt to go under.

But what is a mate? Did that trigamist male Yellow-Green copulate with all three females? I have no way of telling, but I do know that the question is worth raising. On April 18, 1962, Frederick watched a marked male copulate with a marked female on a plowed field. A few days later that same female was consorting with another male—an unmarked one!

We have seen very few copulations on the Buena Vista Marsh, despite literally hundreds of hours' watching, but the case of the female apparently mated to two different males gives food for thought. Fortunately with harriers there are no legal complications regarding establishment of paternity.

The pair bond in harriers began to look far more flexible and imprecise than I had suspected. For convenience, in 1969, I defined the male who brought food to a nesting female, or who was the chief defender of the nest against intruders, as the *mate* at that nest. It is still the best definition I can offer.

By 1969 I had learned a great deal, but not precisely what I was after. My most intriguing finding was that harriers that have reared young successfully tend to return to the study area. It was as though the rearing of young *imprinted* them to return.

To my astonishment, of 112 females that returned to nest on the Buena Vista Marsh in another year, at least 87 had reared young successfully there. Of 61 males, 50 had previous records of success! Harriers that failed to rear young essentially never returned to the marsh.

If only we had managed to catch and color-mark all the breeding harriers! We don't know the whole story, because any time we caught an unbanded adult, it might have had a previous record of success or failure—most likely of success. It is plain that successfully raising young has a profound influence on their "will" to return.

It began to look as though there were an extremely valuable cohort in the breeding population of the Buena Vista Marsh: successful parents. Successful parents not only tended to come back to the study area, but furthermore they tended to be successful in rearing young again. Of seven males who had fledged young the year they were caught, six fledged young again when they came back another year; one of them returned still another year, but this time his nest failed. And of ten females who had fledged young, nine were again successful when they returned. For one of these we had a four-year history: after two successful seasons she failed in the third, but reared young successfully again in the fourth.

We only managed to catch slightly over half of the breeders, but as my mother always used to say, success builds success. This rather small cohort of good parents was contributing an abnormally high number of the young fledged on the study area.

In all the years of this 25-year study only once did a female breed again with the same male, but she wasn't true to him; she mated with another male in another year. It looks as though pair fidelity on the Buena Vista Marsh is the exception, rather than the rule.

It even seemed that there must be a mechanism regulating *against* pair fidelity, but the project was about to take a new direction, and it would be some years before I would return to this particular problem.

At any rate, my hopes were high. I had 92 breeding harriers marked—and answers must be just around the corner.

8 Mice Move into My Life

Voles will play an important role in this story. They are also known as meadow mice, and their genus is *Microtus*. They are about four inches long and look like Lilliputian beavers, except that their little short tails are round rather than flat. They have tiny, beady eyes, and sharp front teeth, with which they ordinarily bite off vegetation for food. Voles make runways in matted grass, and the females build neat little shelters—rather like upside-down birds' nests—for rearing their young.

Voles are fairly closely related to the lemmings, who notoriously suffer from over-population and make dramatic journeys—even into the sea to drown—when population pressure becomes too intense. Voles, however, have not found such a dramatic way out of the dilemma of over-population. About every four years the vole population becomes excessive, then crashes, and it takes about four years for the population to rise again. This is roughly a four-year population cycle.

When the vole population on my study area crashes, it almost seems that these small mammals must have become extirpated. Indeed, when experienced trappers set over a thousand traps and catch only one mouse, the population is low.

No one knows what causes cyclic animal populations to crash: stress of over-crowding? disease? starvation? snow depth? sun spots? Theories abound.

The numbers of voles during the high point of a cycle are so great, that the British term "vole plague" gives the very impression

I get: incredible numbers! Runways are interlaced with runways, voles scuttle across trails and scoot from tussock to tussock in the marsh—and I can catch a substantial number just by hand-grabbing.

In the late 1960s, Daniel Q. Thompson, the vole expert, paid us a visit. Instead of asking, "How are the children?" or exclaiming, "You're looking well," we plunged right into shop talk.

Thompson produced a figure showing his latest vole index in our region: namely, southeastern Minnesota, Wisconsin, and northern Illinois. I gasped.

"Stop, Dan, let me show *you* something!"

I ran to the corner cabinet where I kept my harrier notes, rummaged, and produced a pencilled graph. "Let's put them up against the window. . . . Look at that match! Of course the number of harrier eggs and young fledged are going to have a strong relationship, but look at your voles right along with them!"

Dan, who is not quick to commit himself, muttered, "That certainly is surprising."

"How'd you get your vole index?"

"I've been testing sampling techniques. This graph is based on counting stems cut by voles on sample plots."

After the first flush of excitement, I admitted, "The first year of our graphs held against the window really doesn't fit. We thought we'd covered the study area fairly thoroughly, but 1960 was the first

These sharp front teeth can nicely nip a finger as well as a stem.

year we really managed to." Then I added very thoughtfully, "We couldn't have missed by as much as that. There's got to be another reason."

Dan suggested, "It could be that the voles on the Buena Vista Marsh reacted differently from the rest of the region in 1960."

"Why, Dan, that reminds me of a paper by Hagen. (20) He correlated the number of raptor nests on his study area with abundance of voles, but the voles weren't trapped on his study area—just in the region."

My next statement was to cost me hundreds of hours of my life. "In my study the mice will be trapped right on the study area." I had no inkling what was in store.

Dan gently approached the practical aspects. "Who pays for all this, Fran? Do you have a grant?"

"No, I'm no good at getting them.

"Actually, I'm trying to keep this work rather secret because I'm always afraid that I'll be criticized for spending so much time working on hawks. After all I'm paid to do work on prairie chickens, and chickens are really the main thing."

"But you've got a lot done on your Harrier Project!"

"Dan, I always figure that if the chief of research in the Conservation Department criticizes me for spending so much time working on hawks, I'll look him straight in the face and ask, 'You don't mind if I play bridge in my spare time, do you?

" 'Well, I'm only paid 60 percent of the time and I'd rather trap hawks than play bridge.' "

(Fortunately, this imaginary conversation never came to pass.)

Dan pursued the practical aspects. "I think I can help you. If you can find a good man to run my transects here, and we can get permanent leases on three 40-acre plots of good vole habitat, I can add the Buena Vista Marsh to my study."

Within 24 hours, Dan had hired Paul Drake, selected the permanent mouse plots; and Frederick had arranged for the needed leases.

When spring came, the neighbors were treated to the sight of signs designating Cornell University study plots and to the sight of Paul in the rain, hunkered under a plastic sheet, clipping stems or counting tiny clippings made by mice—and to the sight of endless careful surveying. Some perfectly ordinary-looking 40-acre plots bloomed with 2 rows of plastic markers set 60 feet apart. Two break-

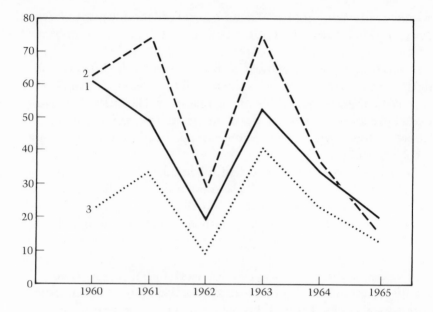

*Harrier productivity in relation to vole abundance, showing: (1) percent of
stems cut by voles in sample plots in Wisconsin, northern Illinois, and
southeastern Minnesota (Daniel Q. Thompson's data); (2) number of harrier eggs on the study area; and (3) number of harriers fledged on the
study area. (25)*

back snap traps were set close to each marker, and if at all possible
each trap was hidden by drawing nearby vegetation over it, so that
no raptor would find a caught mouse and carry the trap away.

I admit I was mighty intolerant of this last precaution: (1) because it made it so very hard to find the traps oneself, and (2) because I deemed it unlikely that any raptor would be apt to carry off
a trap. I was wrong on the second count. In 1981 Dale Gawlik found
one of our mouse traps in a harrier nest! (19)

For three glorious years the Cornell University mouse project
ran the vole index on my harrier study area. I helped Paul Drake,
and later Frank Renn, if I had time. The mouse project was housed
under our roof, but all I really needed to do was to feed whoever
was on the project and reap the benefits of the data collected.

I did find time to worry: all that surveying! running the traps in each carefully measured plot for three nights! How would I ever find time when Cornell could no longer do it?

I devised the Hamerstrom Mouse Index. Using last year's jar of peanut butter for bait, and borrowing Cornell's 120 mouse traps, I looked across each 40-acre mouse plot, picked a straight line— through good representative vole habitat—toward some tall land-mark, such as a white pine; and set the traps one and one-half steps (about eight feet) apart. My results coincided with Cornell's almost to a mouse. Of course, I was just after an index to the population, and not after a real census.

We have continued the Hamerstrom Mouse Index through 1983. It is quick, it is fun, it is cheap, and it is a practical index for showing relative changes in abundance of voles and other small mammals.

The Hamerstrom Mouse Index has hit two snags because the project ran so many years. The original plots were leased with the understanding that they would be left *undisturbed*. Prime vole habitat in central Wisconsin and in many other areas is usually Kentucky bluegrass. Kentucky bluegrass is not native—it was introduced from Europe—but like many native grasses, it only thrives where there is periodic disturbance.

Few people put their minds on how to maintain good mouse habitat; most people just want to get rid of mice. The only way we could have kept the original plots for any kind of mouse count would have been to manage the bluegrass by periodic burning, mowing, plowing, or even fertilizing. In time, the bluegrass on two of our three original plots started to become sparse from lack of disturbance; nettles and spirea began to invade the third. Our solution was simple: we simply selected new plots each year that re-sembled the original plots when they contained much good vole habitat. Fortunately we noticed these changes in time to make re-adjustments.

The second snag surfaced in 1982. The gabboons that were run-ning the mouse trapline came in with ridiculously small catches. I read them the riot act, described good vole habitat, and sent them back out to trap in good bluegrass forties. They continued to return with small catches, so I went out on the marsh with them to try to figure out what was wrong with their technique, and to show them.

Three gabboons and I drove around so I could show them how to select a good forty for trapping. I was pretty smug about it. First I showed them some fields that had recently been good, but where the bluegrass was too thin now. Then—with the utmost confidence—I drove them to fields I expected to be good, and not one field was adequate! By this time the *gabboons* were getting pretty smug . . . and within the hour I found myself apologizing to them!

All the plots worth considering were on land managed for prairie chickens. The state game managers had had poor conditions for controlled burns, so much of the bluegrass was thin. And where the bluegrass should have grown, lush reed canary—a rank grass imported from Europe—was invading prime bluegrass soil.

"All right, then trap in reed canary!" They did, and that's where the voles lurked.

Reed canary is so aggressive in southern Wisconsin that it's becoming a pest—taking over the low prairies. So far the harriers have adapted to moderate reed-canary invasion.

This all points up something rather important: our attitude toward mice and mouse habitat may have to undergo a change. Mice, and particularly voles, are important to some of the species we cherish.

9 *Trouble Coming*

In the late 1960s hawk watching was becoming popular. Masses of people sat on Hawk Mountain in Pennsylvania, Hawk Ridge close to the lake shore at Duluth, Minnesota, and various other lookouts, mostly in the Eastern part of the United States to watch the fall migration. Most of them brought along picnics and hoped that they would not miss the magnificent spectacle of The Big Flight Day. A few dedicated individuals (both professional and amateur) watched day after day, striving for an accurate count of hawks passing by on migration, and the figures they amassed are of considerable interest.

Hundreds of people took to hawk watching, parking lots were established, the traffic on weekends reminded one of the road to a Big League Game, and much publicity was generated.

Hawks like to migrate along flight lines either where winds striking mountain ranges create updrafts for easy travel, or along the western shores of lakes. Many people assume that these are just about the only places worth watching the migration.

Dan Berger, who helped with the Prairie Chicken work for many springs, cannot resist counting hawks. He persuaded Frederick and me to keep track too, so an obscure hawk count—posing no traffic problems—and without the luxury of picnics was started. We kept the count standard: three good observers (usually Frederick, Dan, and I) recorded every hawk we saw in the course of our normal spring field work. We kept the count going for ten years.

Our normal field work started before daybreak. We guided ob-

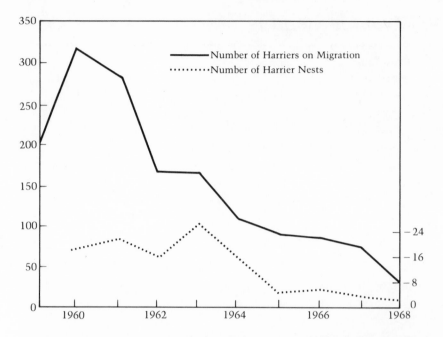

April 3, 1960, was an extraordinary flight day—unlike anything we've seen before or since. Six sharp-shinned hawks, 4 Cooper's hawks, 51 red-tailed hawks, 27 rough-legged hawks, 8 unidentified Buteos, 40 harriers, and 11 kestrels. Even without that big day, 1960 was the top year for harriers seen. The drop in the number of migrants was alarming.

servers to blinds and then watched booming prairie chickens ourselves until about 8:00 a.m. Then we picked up our observers and returned to headquarters. This gave us about five hours to record hawks every morning. Most of our prairie chicken watching was from blinds, and as hawks are attracted to booming prairie chickens, our opportunities for hawk counting were probably enhanced.

The daily hawk count that we had kept up for ten years was not very exciting. It was just a chore that became a habit.

But pesticide stories were mounting. Robins had been found dying in tremors on city lawns, and peregrine falcons were declining sharply east of the Mississippi River and in parts of Europe as well. DDT was the suspected culprit. Just about everybody has a weakness for robins, and peregrine falcons have captured the romantic imagination of man for centuries—but who cared about harriers? Even after Wisconsin passed a law protecting all hawks in the early 1950s, Portage County, where most of my study area lay, still paid a bounty for dead "marsh hawks" brought to the county courthouse.

By 1963 the rumors of DDT's insidious damage had become ominous, and the time had come to try to figure out how harriers were faring. I knew something was wrong with the birds on my study area, but was scarcely prepared for our spring migration counts—the lowest we had ever seen.

There were several other indications that there was something wrong with the harriers on my study area. The birds were listless. They set up weak territories. If we put Ambrose in a weak territory to try to catch some of these non-breeders, they either gave a few half-hearted stoops at the owl or simply flew away.

Listless birds were worrisome. Were they sick? Was it DDT? And how about the non-breeding birds—weren't there too many on the marsh?

Raptor biologists tend to speak of a "floating population"—in-

Dan and Fran disentangle a lucky catch.

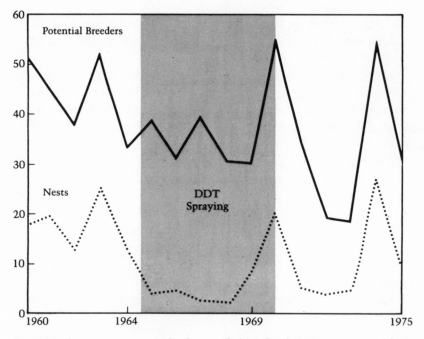

In 1968, the worst year, we had enough females for 20 nests, yet only 2 nested; the rest were listless.

dividuals that fail to breed, but are more or less ready to move in if they have a chance at parenting. I call members of my floating population part of the "potential breeders." The floaters can serve a useful function as a sort of backup team, but too many potential breeders in relation to actual nesters would imply that not enough birds were breeding!

We kept track of potential breeders each year. With two or three people working the Marsh daily we got to know most of the individuals. We often only recognized them by plumage, because we could count on finding the same birds in the same areas day after day. Our count of potential breeders has never been perfect. Two or more of the harrier crew listed all the harriers on a study-area map. The period covered was essentially between June 15 and July 8. All potential-breeder listing was done independently: no fair comparing with another gabboon's list!

Then, after the lists were complete, came the great discussion. The lists were remarkably close every year, and discussions hinged around the presence or absence of very few birds. That doesn't mean

Fran Hamerstrom makes a set with fiberglass zip poles.

Gabboon setting out to trap.

that some of the discussions weren't lively but the total count of brown harriers (females and subadult males), and gray harriers (adult males), came very close. Actually, some of the discussions resolving the potential-breeder count were far from courteous— especially in the early years of the study. What was important was that independent observers had come up with essentially the same number of potential breeders for the Marsh.

We selected June 15 as the starting point because school was out and many gabboons couldn't get to work until then—besides, the spring migration was over. July 8 was selected for the approximate termination date, for a more complex reason relating to nest abandonment and resulting shifts in population. The disobedience of a bunch of farm children tipped us off to this situation.

On May 23, 1961, Dan Berger, my son Alan, and I went in to trap the adults at a nest. We were followed by about six little towheads.

Berger ordered, "Go back to the house where you belong."

Six barefoot children stood perfectly still and then, as soon as we moved towards the nest, they followed us again. They wanted to watch. At last we scared them away, set up the dho-gaza, and caught the male without difficulty. We put up the dho-gaza again and caught the female although the two top corners of the net had failed to break free! It was a lucky catch.

We processed the birds, and marked them with yellow imps, and on our way back past the farmhouse we stopped to give the children a lecture: "Keep away from the nest. If you go back, the eggs won't hatch. There'll be no baby birds. You understand?" The next day no parent birds defended the nest. A well-beaten trail about three feet wide led from the farmhouse to the nest.

At the time I thought it was odd that the parents left the area so soon, but later we found this to be the rule with broken-up nests: the adults normally left the study area within 24 hours of nest abandonment.

By July 8, our termination date, most harriers have set up nesting territories and few nests have been broken up. Large-scale haying will soon be underway. This causes a partial shift in nesting populations: harriers that lose their nests *on* my study area will leave after the mower has done its horrid work, and harriers that have lost their nests *off* the area may well turn up to spend the rest of the summer on the Buena Vista Marsh. July 8, therefore, was the logical termination date for the potential breeder count. This count proved to be a mercy when my population got into trouble. Plainly it *was* in trouble, not because there were too few harriers on my study area, but because they were failing to breed! In the worst year, 1968, we had enough females for 20 nests, yet only two nested; the study area, but because they were failing to breed!

So two signals gave me the clue that something was very wrong. Not only were too few migrants passing through in spring, but how about those listless potential breeders that failed to nest?

It also became harder to catch the adults, as listless birds are not aggressive. Banding was essential to document what was happening in this emergency. Our equipment had to become progressively more sophisticated.

And in later years, most trapping was before sunup when the net was less visible. Besides, males tended to be harder to catch than females, so if we set up early enough, we might net the male before the female even left the nest!

Trapping a weakened harrier population was indeed a challenge. We gave our best efforts to finding out what was wrong.

10 Death of the Sky-Dance

Sometimes it is good to write about certain things long after they have happened. They cause less pain, and one sees them in perspective. Sky-dancing disappeared and only gradually returned after the DDT period. Even so it is difficult to write about it now because it brings me back to those miserable years when there was so little hope.

Starting in 1937 I have spent most of my springs on the marshes of central Wisconsin. It wouldn't be nice if the first robin of spring didn't arrive, but for me it was more unthinkable not to see the harrier—hawk of the marshes, swift twisting on silvery wings as he danced over sere meadows against lead-blue skies.

I think back to my early notes and to those birds that started my pair-fidelity study. I think of lying alone on ditch banks in the sun, after the prairie chickens had left their booming grounds . . . April sun beating on my skin after the long winter. I lay on the ditch banks to delight in the varied styles of sky-dancing males—lazily making mental notes. It never occurred to me that someday those lazy mental notes would be my only record.

Sky-dancing has been described by many observers. Mr. Broley, in Bent's *Life Histories of North American Birds of Prey* (1937) (3) wrote:

> This is a vigorous and pleasing series of nose dives, mostly done by the male, although the female frequently takes part in them. This takes place sometimes at an altitude of 500 feet,

but the usual flight averages 60 feet up, swooping down to 10 feet from the ground. It might be illustrated by placing a number of capital U's together as UUUUUUUUUUUUUUUUUU, as the turn at the bottom is well rounded out, but at the apex the bird almost stalls, tipping downward again to continue the movement. Some observers claim it makes a somersault as it turns, but only on one occasion have I seen any indication of this. The wings are kept fully extended during the whole period, and they appear to be working easily all the time. I have seen a male make 71 of these dips in succession, fly on for a short distance and commence anew. The average number of dips would be perhaps 25. The flight is frequently made while the female is flying along near the ground hunting for mice, below the male, or again he may swoop continually in one location while she is standing on the ground. The movement is extremely graceful and is a welcome sight each spring.

Forbush (18) gave this rather imaginative description in 1929: "The courtship of the Marsh Hawk is carried on largely in its favorite element. In warm spring days a pair may be seen soaring to a great height, when one will suddenly plunge far downward and turn a complete forward or sidelong somersault in the air. Sometimes one falling thus from a height will turn over and over again in the manner of a tumbler pigeon. As it bounds up and down in the air, it seems to move more like a rubber ball than a bird."

Temme (44) gives a fascinating diagram of the sky-dance on the North Sea island of Norderney. I translate, "At the highest point of each orbital tour there is a quick reversal so that the bird flies more or less up-side down. Thereafter the bird swings way down and utilizes the impetus for the next roll."

Breckenridge (10) gives one of the best descriptions:

Soon after the arrival of the birds on their nesting grounds, the courting birds, mainly the males, engage in remarkable aerial maneuvers. . . . These acrobatics have been described by a number of well known observers as somersaults (Seton, 1885; Roberts, 1932). Throughout these two seasons' observations and those of a number of previous years, the writer has never observed what could rightly be called a somersault, although the bird does turn upside down during the maneuver. The bird, in a very evident state of excitement, dived from a height of about seventy-five feet at a very steep angle for perhaps fifty feet, when it "zoomed" up again to about the original height where it turned over *sidewise* like the wings of a wing nut being

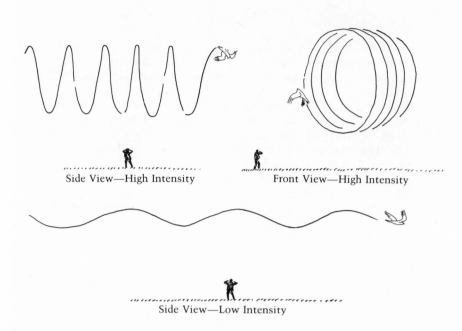

Side View—High Intensity   Front View—High Intensity

Side View—Low Intensity

A sky dance.

turned onto a bolt. The aviator refers to this as a "barrel roll." Individuals were seen to turn over either to the right or to the left, to the right, however, was much the commoner turn. In this inverted position the bird beat its wings two or three times, then righted itself by the same sidewise turn, generally in the reverse direction, and again dived into the great dip to repeat the performance again and again.

At first when I read all these accounts, it seemed as though they had been written at different times of year, or the writers were in different moods. And then, when sky-dancing disappeared and I needed to describe classic sky-dancing to the gabboons so they could recognize it, I realized that the authors of these accounts had watched from different vantage points! Plainly the classic sky-dance has a different look depending on where you are when you watch it.

For a moment I would like to get ahead of my story. Even after my population recovered from the DDT years, classic sky-dancing failed to reappear until about 1980! Possibly it is a learned behavior, and there may not have been enough teachers left alive to bring it back sooner.

Be that as it may, in 1965, for the first time in 24 springs in central Wisconsin, I did not *once* see a harrier sky-dance, either during the nesting season or on migration.

We had never recorded the number of sky-dancing males on the Buena Vista Marsh. The sight was so common; some mornings we must have seen 10 or 12 dancing in 16 miles of travel—and sometimes three harriers sky-dancing over one meadow. It was after sky-dancing stopped that we wished we had kept records.

We never recorded transfers either. They were so common and we never dreamed their style would change. Male harriers have a special way of flying when they are about to transfer prey. They travel high—in a straight line—and once recognized, the sight of a male on a direct path means he's carrying, and almost certainly headed for a nesting area.

In what I consider the classic transfer, the male flies high over the nest, the female comes up, the male drops the prey, and the female swings gracefully beneath him and catches the food in the air.

Every now and then the male drops, not one, but *two* prey items and the female is seldom successful in catching both. The most unsuccessful transfer I ever saw was one summer when the gabboons were having great difficulty in finding a nest on Hanson's farm. I thought I'd show them.

By chance I saw an adult male in direct flight about a mile from this territory as I was driving home from shopping. I floored the accelerator and managed to keep up with him. He rose even higher as he reached the Hanson meadow; I scrambled up on the cartop carrier in time to see the female swing high to receive the prey. It was a good moment; all I needed to do was to keep my binoculars on her—or so I thought. The prey, a blackbird, fell a foot or two, got its bearings, and buzzed off into space. . . .

My chance to show how quickly I could find a nest was ruined by that lucky blackbird. Furthermore it was the only time that any of us witnessed an attempted transfer of a living creature.

Throughout the years I had noticed that different males had somewhat different styles of dropping prey to their mates, and now and again I had watched the female come up so close that the transfer was almost talon-to-talon. But in the mid-1960s, rough, grabby talon-to-talon transfers low to the ground became common! Don Follen, Sr., who was censusing hawks about 40 miles west of my study area, told me he also was seeing many almost frantic talon-to-

It's a sky show, and normally the transfer is successful.

talon transfers, often involving crabbing. Some people associate crabbing with crabby old women, but in hawks it is actual sparring. Sometimes the males didn't seem to want to let go of the food at all.

This was complicated by a unique development: *robber females*. Robber females—and we have no evidence that any of them had nests during the DDT years—tried to snatch food from males carrying prey.

Decline of migrants, weak territorial defense, the disappearance of sky-dancing, frantic talon-to-talon transfers, and even robber females were all straws in the wind that something was very wrong. But the decline in numbers of nests on the Buena Vista Marsh was staggering.

All populations have their ups and downs. I needed to know about normal fluctuations in a harrier population so I wrote to Eddie Balfour, on the island of Orkney, to find out how much the number of nests on his 13-square-mile study area fluctuated from year to year. He kindly sent me his counts from 1944 through 1965 so I got a 21-year comparison with a closely related race.

The first time I saw a DDT spray plane I gasped, because I thought it was a Conservation Department pilot who was supposed to be spraying brush with herbicides to improve prairie chicken

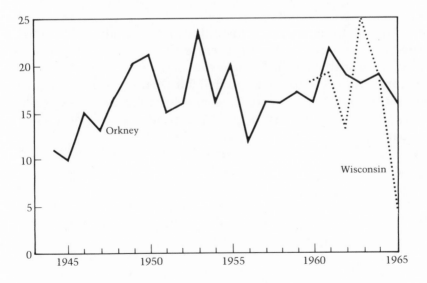

Balfour's population certainly fluctuated, but he never had an ominous drop like mine. (1, 2, 25)

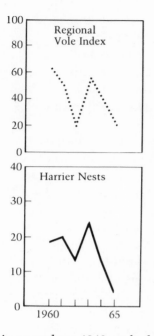

As recently as 1963 we had had 25 nests, and now, in 1968, we were down to two.

habitat (it was in the mid-60s). Instead the pilot was flying low over a bawling herd of cattle, sloshing them with some kind of spray until they were fairly drenched. The owner of the cows was a friend of mine, and I rushed to his house to find out what was going on and to try to put this misdemeanor in as good light as I could. (After all, I was a Conservation Department biologist and it was my duty to do what I could.)

Mr. Lundberg was out by the barn tinkering with a tractor.

"What," I cried with considerable agitation, "is going on in your south pasture?"

Mr. Lundberg is a gentle person and soft-spoken. "It's all right, Mrs. Hamerstrom. The cattle will settle down pretty soon."

"Is that one of the Department pilots?"

Mr. Lundberg laid down a wrench. "The flies are terrible this year."

"Flies?" I couldn't make the connection.

Mr. Lundberg paused so he wouldn't have to shout over the roar of the plane as it turned near the barn before taking another swing at the unhappy dairy herd. "Flies," he resumed. "I *hired* that plane to spray my cows."

For a moment I was too astonished to ask another question. At last I said, "What are they spraying with?"

"DDT. It keeps the flies off."

Before long I was to hear an interesting statement: Mother's milk in many regions is so heavily contaminated with DDT that if it were a commercial product it would be barred from interstate shipment. Ho hum: the dairy herd getting it directly.

I never saw cattle sprayed with DDT again. It was an isolated instance.

Spray rigs on the ground had applied DDT to crops in our area for some years, but it was not until 1964 that aerial spraying of crops increased dramatically and my harrier population got into difficulties.

11 But They Don't Lay Eggs

Whilst these many things were happening to my harriers there were other, nationally publicized developments in the pesticide story. Most of the groups involved in researching the use of DDT have received credit. It was Professor J. J. Hickey of the University of Wisconsin who launched the big attack. The alarming decline of the peregrine falcon east of the Mississippi River first tuned him in to the trouble.

Hickey is not a falconer, but he said to me, "Fran, it may be that the knowledge held by a handful of falconers may save the peregrine falcon." He was so right. I am a falconer. The general public is totally unaware of the vast debt they owe to falconers. It was falconers who first alerted Hickey to the decline, falconers who first found pesticide residues in the peregrines in the Arctic; and later—it was falconers who successfully bred the big falcons in captivity and developed techniques for reestablishing them in the wild!

Even Professor Hickey, who recognized the need for action, didn't realize the part that falconers were to play. In 1964 he said, "Fran, I'm going to assemble an international peregrine symposium. Here are the names of eleven top peregrine researchers as a start. Maybe I should invite a falconer too?"

I looked at his list of eleven and said, "Joe dear, of your list of eleven top researchers, eight are falconers—and five are *distinguished* falconers!"

As harriers are not normally flown in falconry, advice from

falconers and peregrine researchers about thin eggshells wasn't
much use to me. And advice was pouring in from many quarters:
"Fran, collect eggs. You've got to look for eggshell thinning."

"Look," I'd answer in exasperation, "harriers are different from
peregrines! They are short-stopped before laying by aberrant behavior. Most of them are not laying eggs!"

I'd add, "You want me to find out if they are laying thin-shelled
eggs? Most of them aren't laying *any*. They're listless."

"Fran, shoot some of your harriers. You've got to be tough and
take action to save the population! Send some bodies in to a lab for
analysis."

"There's got to be a better way," I muttered to myself. "It's got
to be biopsy."

Dan Berger and Jim Enderson were ahead of me. Berger—and
I noticed his fingers trembled quite a lot cutting into a hawk, for
he has a deep love of hawks—showed me how they conducted
biopsies.

The technique is remarkably simple; I preferred to use manicure scissors. And I was very glad that nobody had persuaded me to
shoot some of my few breeding harriers.

The next question that arose was: Should I take fat samples? or
muscle samples? Ian Prestt and Derek Ratcliffe, the famous British
researchers, urged me to take muscle samples as a more reliable
evaluation of the bird's contamination. American researchers, however, depended on fat samples, and if I were to compare my work
with theirs, fat samples were plainly indicated. Fat would lie just
under the skin, and would be more easily reached, but I had experience: a minor in veterinary medicine and—more importantly, in
this instance—I had started what I called my "Wild Animal Hospi-
tal" when I was 11 years old, where I had to operate to keep animals
alive.

I could take either fat or muscle; the problem was to pick the
more useful technique. It didn't take me long to solve the problem:
no male harrier had enough fat on him for a useful sample. Defending the nests and carrying food apparently kept them slimmed-
down. Some of the females did have enough fat. They had recently
stopped incubating, and incubation is probably the laziest period in
a female harrier's life. (About all she has to do is to keep the eggs
warm and have food brought to her. She uses this lazy period to advantage by molting some of her major flight feathers.) I suspect that

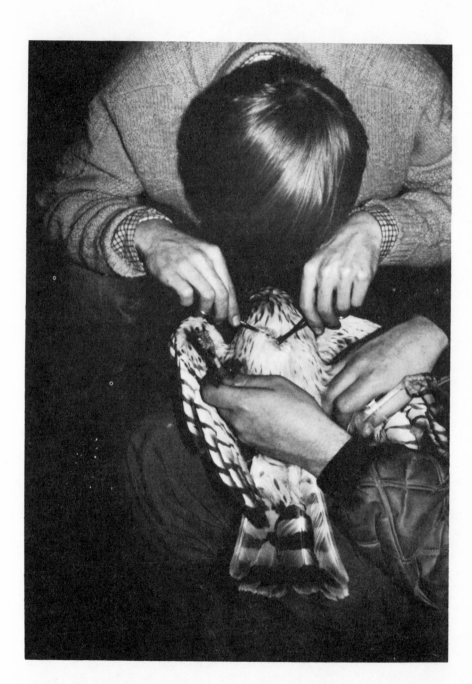

Making the incision for biopsy. This is a red-jessed bird that returned to the Marsh to breed again.

some monogamous females and favored "wives" in harrier harems actually put on fat during incubation.

Be that as it may, as none of the males had enough fat for laboratory samples, mine would be based on muscle. I had no intention of using different techniques for different sexes.

The sample needed was about half the size of a pea. First I pushed aside the feathers, wetting them to keep them out of the way. Then I cut the skin, and with my manicure scissors—which I kept sharpened for the first time in my life—I made two quick cuts so I could lift out my muscle sample. Then I sewed the incision back up with three to five stitches. The bird was already weighed, banded, jessed, and processed, except for one more step. Just before release I imped the bird, in part so the bright feathers would let me know how it fared. It was a delight to watch them go right back to dive-bombing the owl, or feeding their young.

Some years later, in 1974, L. G. Frank of the University of Aberdeen gave a paper at the Raptor Research Foundation meeting in Sioux Falls. (33) He described his biopsy techniques which involved putting the bird under with an anesthetic, and then holding it at least 40 minutes in a recovery cage.

"Do you think all that's necessary?" I asked.

The discussion at the meeting was lively, but when we got together during the coffee break it was even livelier.

"Look, your birds are woozy for almost an hour after you biopsy, and mine are up and about their business within minutes!

It's like going to the dentist," I added. "When that dentist leans over you and asks, 'Would you like me to give you a little something?' I know that if he gives me 'a little something,' the side of my jaw will be swollen for hours, and it will put me at a strong disadvantage—especially if I have to give a lecture or something of the sort. I need to get back on the job. So do my harriers!"

"I can see," he allowed, "that with breeding birds you have no option."

Looking at the whole picture from the viewpoint of a hawk, I think a speedy biopsy followed by a quick release would be preferable to waking up woozy in a recovery cage. Harriers minded my holding their wings for imping more than they minded having me cut into their chests.

As soon as the muscle tissue had been removed, it was wrapped in sterile aluminum foil or put in a sterile vial, and then we put it

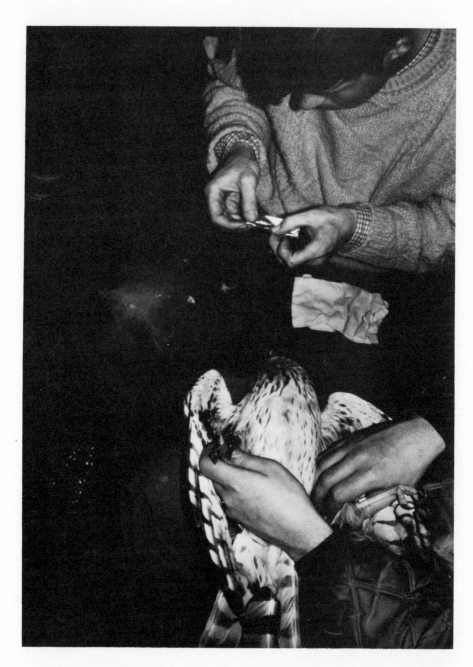

Putting the sample in aluminum foil.

next to "blue ice"—that useful commercial product that keeps things cool without getting them wet. After that we bundled this precious little package in a winter parka and drove back to headquarters as fast as possible. The samples went into the freezer compartment of our refrigerator, next to packages of fish, deer meat, ducks, and vegetables.

Few laboratories were analyzing samples of DDT and other environmental contaminants at that time. Where should I send them?

12   *Fund Raising*

Money. Nobody paid me to work on harriers. Financing the project was always a problem. Frederick had stated that it would be easier on the family finances if what I wanted was merely yachts, diamonds, and furs . . . rather than a houseful of bearded gabboons.

In the 25 years of my Harrier Project, the only outright cash that I received was $300 from the Josselyn Van Tyne Research Fund of the Wilson Ornithological Society in 1960, and a $1,000 Frank M. Chapman grant of the American Ornithologists' Union in 1964. I am very grateful for both . . . and especially to Frederick, who is a generous and patient man.

If I had the knack for getting grants, I would simply have picked up the phone, found the best lab for pesticide analyses, offered to pay for the results, and my life might have been simpler. (It is my impression that the rich lead simpler and duller lives.) As it was, my friend Joe Hickey was about to come to my rescue—he who led the investigation of DDT's part in the decline of the peregrine falcon.

At the international raptor-DDT symposium which he organized in Madison, Wisconsin in 1965 there were some pretty lively discussions that never got into the transactions. At this point two camps were lining up for battle: Hickey, Lucille Stickel of Patuxent Wildlife Research Center, and Ian Prestt and Derek Ratcliffe of the British Nature Conservancy were amassing evidence aplenty that DDT was the culprit; but agri-industry experts persistently downplayed the clear evidence that DDT was contaminating the environment. Fifty participants, from eight countries, sat at tables with six at each table. We all concentrated; there were no little groups talking about other things in the hallways. I will never forget one electric moment. A man from the back of the room jumped to his feet and, ignoring the chairman, pressed past the tables to the podium almost shouting his message, "My name is Rice, J. N. I am sick and tired of all this brain-washing by the Federal Government!"

I was interpreter for German and French at that symposium and Frederick was to write the ecological appraisal. We both had our hands full and had had little time to study the famous people sharing our table. The Stickels sat straight in their chairs. Lucille Stickel, who was a federal employee, looked prepared to interrupt the proceedings and do battle at any moment. Prestt looked amiable, but I rather suspect he missed nothing. Ratcliffe never cracked a smile; his demeanor was funereal—like a grave-digger's in front of the bereaved family.

"I am sick and tired of all this brain-washing by the Federal Government." Rice's declaration brought abrupt silence in the room. Then Ratcliffe giggled. His somber face contorted; he tried to suppress helpless gasps of laughter. Prestt and Lucille Stickel got the giggles too, and sounds of uncontrolled laughter emerged from our table off and on for the rest of the session. It showed what a great strain those of us who were uncovering the case against DDT were under.

We are confronted with similar conflicts between "saving the economy" and preserving the environment today. Rice, J. N. had put the problem in a nutshell in 1965.

The conflict was to make difficulties for my Harrier Project. It may have had a part in my inability to get grants, and it certainly made it difficult for me to get information.

This symposium and *Peregrine Falcon Populations: their Biology and Decline*, (35) edited by J. J. Hickey, had a tremendous impact on the scientific community. And it was J. J. Hickey who arranged for money so some of my biopsy samples could be analyzed by the Wisconsin Alumni Research Foundation (WARF). So I learned that the DDT and associated residues in my harriers were as high as those in the British peregrine falcon population when it went into disastrous decline. The symptoms were different. Peregrines were laying soft-shelled eggs that didn't hatch. But as I have said, my harriers were short-stopped by behavioral anomalies before laying eggs.

Harrier Band Recoveries

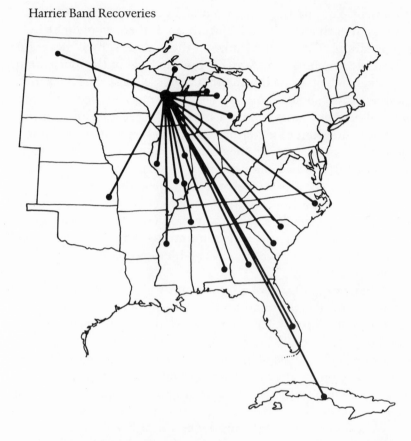

Cotton was said to be one of the most heavily sprayed crops. People don't eat cotton, so if growers figured, "If a little DDT is good, more might be better," there was no one to dissuade them from putting on more. My birds tended to move toward the cotton belt.

We never found a really soft-shelled harrier egg, although the eggs of some of my stronger breeders were a little thin. Daniel Anderson, an expert on the relationship between eggshell thinning and DDT contamination, measured the shells for me.

I wanted to know where my harriers were picking up their DDT. The death of the sky-dance and the listlessness of my returning migrants suggested that the trouble might be right on my study area.

I decided next to biopsy migrants and see how their residues compared with my breeding population.

I have watched harriers in winter swinging past columnar cacti. But these may nest farther west.

Actually I had two reasons for biopsying spring migrants. Those listless birds that didn't breed probably carried high residues; I couldn't catch them defending nests, but they still managed to eat! My plan was to catch them in spring with bait birds, biopsy them, and imp them, so if they hung around as lethargic non-breeders, I'd know what their residues were. It was a nice plan. In 1969 the new gabboon on the project caught 10, but something went wrong with his imping technique! Unidentified non-breeders—with gaps in their wings showing where the imps had fallen out—displayed list-lessness that could not be correlated with their residues because they were no longer color-marked. It was frustrating.

This same gabboon, Rodd Friday, realizing how much he'd messed up the study, came again the next spring and did a splendid job of catching, biopsy, and imping. His catch was of migrants only. Alas, they all moved on within a few weeks and we never saw them again.

The "early birds" caught in the spring of 1970 and 1971 carried substantial residues (see Appendix).

The freezing compartment in the refrigerator amassed more and more biopsy samples. It was staggering to think how much it cost to trap each harrier—the man-hours, and the gas mileage, and incidentals. It was even more staggering to contemplate the cost of having the samples analyzed.

Paul Degurse of our own department—the Wisconsin Department of Natural Resources—who was intensely interested in my findings, offered to get samples run for me. Mysteriously, the samples run in his lab recorded no DDT and no DDD—only DDE, a break-down product of DDT. Neither he nor I could ever account for this, but DDE levels were those often used for comparison. I didn't know where to turn next. Dr. Stickel of Patuxent gave me little hope, and WARF's prices were $25 per sample. It doesn't sound like much money nowadays, but the Project had no funds at all!

One morning, as I sat at my desk working up some rather dif-ficult prairie chicken population data, I heard somebody in my kitchen. I quit tabulating, stomped into the kitchen and not to my surprise I found a well-muscled young man with a beard. His field clothes had a certain California-style elegance, but I was busy, so I simply said, "Go down to the machine shed and look at the eagles." I figured he was a hawk trapper from somewhere.

Sending people down to look at the eagles was a sure thing. It always gave me a chance to go on with my work. That morning was an exception. The chap asked me a question. He asked me more questions—penetrating ones about pesticides. I thought, "Good Lord! This chap's got a brain."

Lunchtime came and I invited him to stay. (Frederick is accustomed to my impulsive invitations.) We had a rather sketchy meal, but we had my lemon meringue pie for dessert.

I hadn't caught his name, but by suppertime he was still asking me questions. I was learning much from them and starting to fire some back. I invited him to supper. We had a warmed-up mulligan for the main course, and I heated up a wild plum-and-apple pie for dessert.

"Pie," he murmured. "I have never eaten anything like your pies. . . .

"I'll make a deal," he continued, "I'll have my lab analyze as many samples as you want to send and trade you even-Steven for pies."

Thus it came to pass that I met an eccentric bachelor who was gone on my pies. It was Dr. Robert Risebrough—a top expert on DDT!

The standard charge for analyzing residues mounted from $25 to $55. But at this point it behooves me to tell you how I shipped pies to Berkeley, California. Delicate crust is important, and only real lard or bear fat manages the right texture.

I baked pies in the cheapest pie plates I could get at the dime store. After they were baked, I covered them with aluminum foil. Then I slipped them into a worn-out nylon stocking. I selected a

big cardboard box, and fastened the toe of the stocking to the middle of one side and the top of the stocking to the other side of the box—so the pie would hang, gently, as in a hammock.

I would like to acknowledge the help of Peter and Carolyn Conners, who actually ran my biopsies in Risebrough's lab, and also that of an eccentric bachelor, who taught me a great deal.

Risebrough's attitude toward my data and mine were very different. He was delighted that I had noticed changes in the behavior of my harriers, but he wanted to lump my findings. I, on the other hand, wanted to correlate severity of contamination with individual birds—marked birds whom I had come to know. I had good case histories for some of these birds and knew how many young they'd fledged; I knew their mates, their weights—and many things about their behavior.

I realize now that I only knew the strongest ones—the breeders. It is entirely possible that those that failed to breed may well have been in a class by themselves—the most heavily contaminated.

13   *Eco-snooping*

"Eco-snooping" was the name we gave to the attempts to find out what was being sprayed on my study area. I first tried something far more straightforward. Although I knew that the chaps at our local Ag Station were known to detest hawks and it was said years ago that they shot them on sight, I paid them a visit. I asked, "What insecticides are the farmers spraying their crops with?"

The answer gave me the first inkling that the work cut out for me was going to deal with a startling diversity of viewpoints and be more like a detective story than I had ever supposed.

"Come into the office." A man with a face well tanned, except for the white forehead characteristic of people who do their outdoor work with hats on, waved me to the visitor's chair. He seated himself behind a desk. "There's a lot of talk about how much DDT is being sprayed."

I nodded.

"A lot of the good farmers come here for advice."

I nodded again.

"If they put too much on, there's a chance that their crops'll be condemned."

I wanted to ask him how big the chance was, but I kept silent.

"Nobody tells me what they put on, nor how much. And a lot of farmers never come in here. I don't know."

He sighed, and started to get out of his chair. "Now I have a question for you.

"You're Mrs. Hamerstrom—the one who catches all those

hawks and lets them go."

I nodded.

"Why do you let them go?"

The spray pilots often ate at the local truck stop. It was no problem for me to slide onto a stool next to a pilot; it was no problem for me to get him talking, even about the danger of his work. But it was impossible for me to find out what he was spraying on corn, beans, and potatoes. Pilots either had instructions not to divulge this information, or—more likely—it simply didn't interest them.

Airstrips appeared. They were all near roads, but not near enough so that we could read the labels on the containers stacked near the planes. I enlisted the help of the gabboons.

"Any time any of you are near an airstrip after dark, it would be nice if you'd just sneak in with a flashlight and copy the labels on some of those cans. Don't use too much light."

Gabboons delight in such assignments.

A former gabboon from the early snowy owl research years paid us a visit and started for home late at night.

"Tom," I said, "do you want to do us a favor on the way

Spray plane with pesticide containers.

home—you'll be going right by an airstrip. If it's not too much trouble, copy the labels on the containers and let me know by mail what you've found." A few days later his report arrived—and with a postscript: "I pasted a sticker on the spray plane! BAN DDT."

We all thought this was very funny.

A few weeks later the whole crew came in from the morning's field work and said, "Guess what we saw! There's a burned spray plane on one of the strips."

"Burned?"

"Yup, there's nothing left of it."

Another gabboon added, "It was the same strip where the 'Ban DDT' sticker was put."

Gabboons are not stupid.

It took me a moment to absorb all this. I called Frederick in from his study to give my words more weight. "From now on no more snooping near the airstrips. I wouldn't want to have to explain to your families how you happened to get shot."

We never learned how that plane happened to burn, and from that day forth I sometimes put on dark clothes, armed myself with a pen light, and copied labels on containers. I kept these little excursions secret from Frederick and the gabboons, and hid my eco-snoop notebook so they wouldn't find it and want to come too. I hid it so well that I haven't found it to this day.

Sometimes I forgot about DDT and savored the beauty of the Marsh.

Perhaps the most glorious time of day on the Marsh is soon after sunrise when frost has chilled the night air in mid-June.

Prairie chicken cocks, stimulated by the drop in temperature, boom, and the melodious sound of their booming rolls over the meadows. Upland sandpipers sit up on fence posts and jacksnipe winnow over willows.

One morning a bittern thunder-pumped. Then a gray harrier flew low over the pale-green willows. I swung the scope and tripod out of the car and followed his path.

A brown female flew up beneath him—and then higher to grapple in a desperate talon-to-talon transfer. And as I watched a spray plane flew across my path of vision. . . .

What would be left if DDT still held sway?

14 *The Road to Recovery*

Now that I look back on the late 1960s, it seems that some curious quirk in my character made me keep up the mouse trapping.

I had learned one thing that I needed to know: Dan Thompson's regional vole index didn't always match mine as exactly as I had first supposed. But I had a cross-check for two important years. My friend Don Follen, Sr., who lived in Arpin, only 40 miles west, confirmed my 1963 vole high followed by a sharp drop in 1964—by rolling hay bales! In 1963 he rolled 25 bales and uncovered 12 voles; while in 1964, 375 bales yielded only 7.

It looked as though I had *proven* that lots of voles do not necessarily make for lots of harrier nests, but I kept the traplines going.

Luck is often involved in research. I'm convinced that if my vole index had involved the tedious surveying of sample plots and running each trap station for three nights, I'd have been looking for a way to get out of it. But the Hamerstrom Mouse Index was fun, and gabboons often vied for a chance to run the line.

Besides, I was stubbornly riding a hunch—but not until 1979, when I was invited to give a paper in Germany, did I get busy and update my chart of vole abundance and harrier nests.

I was amazed at what I had to tell. Plainly all that mouse trapping had paid off: after the dark days of the DDT period, the number of harrier nests on my study area again corresponded with my vole index. The closeness of the relationship was almost spooky.

Two aspects of my chart puzzled me. DDT was banned in

1970, so why did my harriers respond to mouse abundance as early as 1969? It didn't make sense.

My friend Sergej Postupalsky unearthed the answer for me in two obscure publications. (13, 37) These papers showed that the use of DDT in Wisconsin had decreased by about 90 percent just *before* it was banned in 1970. I further learned that the reason for the reduction was because insects were building up immunity to DDT, and DDT residues in some crops made them unsaleable for human consumption. (It seems to me that newspapers could have made headlines of these findings. They didn't. Only the intensely interested and persistent could manage to ferret them out.)

I looked at my chart again. My harrier population seemed to make an instant recovery! There certainly was evidence that recovery from DDT would be very slow indeed. It took me a little while to solve this mystery. The problem was that I considered the harriers on the Buena Vista Marsh *my* harrier population. But my reliable old breeders weren't the only harriers on the Marsh—especially not during vole highs. There was a gypsy cohort that came in to take advantage of meadow mouse abundance. I don't like to call this cohort a "floating population" because "gypsy" strikes me as a more apt term. The gypsy cohort moves about and, like gypsies, pauses where pickings are good.

It would be interesting to find out how the gypsies find a place with plenty of voles. And it wouldn't be very expensive to get some notion of how this comes about. One could learn a lot by trapping a few harriers less than a year old in their wintering areas in the South, putting radios on them, and following their route northwards to study how they found a vole-rich nesting area.

Of course, the radios would have to be placed on birds so young that they had never nested before, or one might waste effort on following a harrier that was "happily" homing to a place where it had successfully reared young in the past.

Until I have evidence to the contrary, I shall assume that my gypsy cohort consists of young who have not nested before, parents whose nests have failed, and possibly some birds that fail to breed for one reason or another. The police have trouble keeping tabs on gypsies, and I have trouble keeping tabs on mine too.

I must admit that if a young harrier were radioed while wintering in Florida, for example, there would be a slight possibility—a very slight possibility—that the youngster was heading "home" to

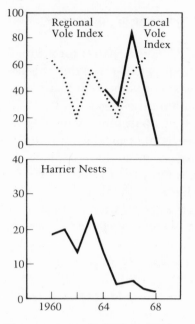

The massive vole high in 1966 certainly had not produced a corresponding increase in numbers of harrier nests.

the area in which it had been hatched. We have banded 647 nestling harriers; on these only 13 were known to return to my study area, and only 10 of these returned to breed.

Throughout the study we have managed to mark over half of our breeding population. One of the disheartening aspects of the DDT period is that I lost essentially all my marked breeders—in fact, all but one. It was *gypsy* harriers that gave my chart the seeming instant recovery after the black DDT years. Heaven only knows where they came from. They found their way to a place where myriads of voles scurried in grass-lined tunnels, clipped stems for food, and reproduced.

By 1965, we had found 99 nests, and 92 of my breeding adults were marked. Perhaps I am a biologist of the old school, but I am firmly convinced that a good study of population dynamics must depend on marked individuals. The recent trend toward computerized habitat evaluation strikes me as a poor substitute—perhaps

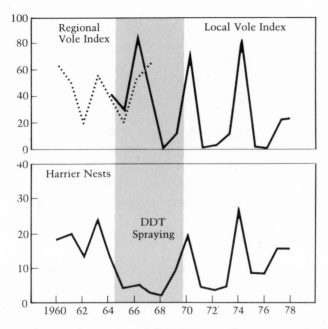

Heavy aerial spraying with DDT started on my area in 1964; the use of DDT was banned in Wisconsin in 1970. Only in the big vole high in 1966 did my harriers fail to respond to this potent mouse!

utilized by those who cannot catch the species they are working on to mark individuals.

The DDT period swept my marked population away. One fascinating bird—the Rosenthal female—made the transition until 1968.

The Rosenthal family lived in a square brick house surrounded by pastures, meadows, and a cornfield or two. A swale ran through the low-lying meadow to the west. In spring wild honeybees dusted their striped abdomens with pussy willow pollen, as they filled their vivid yellow honey bags. And high above their heads a male harrier danced in the sky.

I believe it is the female harrier who actually selects the nest site. (The male often carries nesting material to various spots within the territory. The British call these "cock nests," and their purpose is little understood.)

The Rosenthal female, unlike most other females, had very little choice as to where to put her nest, for the pussy willow swale was isolated. Normal farm practices tended to keep the surrounding vegetation too short for safe nesting. So she could choose: either put her nest in the small swale where she had successfully raised families, or move to a likely-looking spot some distance away. She chose the swale.

I have no idea how many years she had nested in that swale before she was first caught on July 19, 1963.

She was hard to catch; I left Chuck Sindelar with an owl and trapping equipment and came back about an hour later. My first reaction was delight when I drove up to our meeting place. Both birds were in tubes. He had caught the Rosenthal female and her mate. Chuck was lying under a jack pine: he had sunstroke—and when Chuck looks sick he looks very, very sick.

He still had spunk enough to try to order me about. "Process those birds."

I handed him a moistened piece of paper towel and weighed, measured, jessed, imped, etc., as fast as I could.

"She kept knocking down the net," he murmured.

I could picture him—alone—over and over again running through the grasses and goldenrod—running with all his might in the terrible heat of that July day. He did it! He caught the Rosenthal female.

Her iris had only 5 percent brown flecks so she must have been at least two years old. That year she laid four eggs and reared four young.

Now we move deeper into the DDT period. In 1964, she laid four eggs and reared three young.

In 1965 we did not see her on the marsh. Was she gone?

In 1966 she was back, but did not nest.

In 1967 we didn't see her.

In 1968 there were only two nests on my whole study area. It appeared that only the very strongest birds were still able to breed. The Rosenthal female was one of the two. This time she only laid three eggs and reared just two young.

It is hard to get a good case history of a bird as wild and shy as a harrier. Pesticide residues taken at random are useful, but it is good to know more about the individual bird.

The Rosenthal female's nest defense in 1968 was weak. On June 16 she flew around very little. On June 29, we watched her from 9:35 till 10:40. Then she disappeared. She had carried grass in her beak to the nest, landed on three different bushes, and screamed repeatedly. There were spray planes in the distance frequently.

We were determined to catch her, to get her residues, and tried with Ambrose on July 12, 13, and 26. As this did not work we resorted to bal-chatris, baited with starlings, set along a fence west of the nest. On July 28 we finally caught her on one of the bal-chatris. Her residues are given in the Appendix.

The notebook also states, "All slept. Dale 17 hours!!!! Rosenthal effort played a part in this."

I never saw the Rosenthal female again after 1968. The swale is gone; the Rosenthals no longer run a family farm, and agri-industry operators demolished the swale for levelling.

But gypsies appear each spring, especially when voles are abundant, and my cohort of marked breeders has built up again. Thanks to lands under prairie chicken management, the future of harriers on the Buena Vista Marsh looks brighter.

15   *Cruising Range of a Harrier Pair*

It was not until 1972 that the Harrier Project got its first girl gabboon. Frederick found it a refreshing change. It was nice to have a slender girl with long, dark brown hair come into his study from time to time to offer him a cup of coffee. Quite a change from the men.

I put her in charge of telemetry. The imped harriers had given me some idea how far a nesting pair ranged in its hunting, but it was time to map the movements of parents hunting to feed their young. For one thing it would be nice to learn, but the main reason I wanted to know was to learn how near fields sprayed with pesticides they were apt to be hunting.

The College of Natural Resources of the University of Wisconsin/Stevens Point kindly offered me telemetry equipment for the summer—a magnificent present for which I am duly grateful.

Their technician suggested cutting a hole in the roof of my VW bus and its cartop carrier. I said, "No!"

"How," he asked, "can the operator of the vehicle turn the antenna?"

"By shouting orders.

"Deann, the girl gabboon, will be supplied with two junior sub-gabboons who will rotate the antenna when she tells them to." Thus it was that the inhabitants of the Buena Vista Marsh were to be treated to an unusual sight: two boys clinging on top of my VW bus like monkeys—prepared to manipulate the antenna at a moment's notice.

The first job was to align the antenna with the points of the compass. Junior sub-gabboons perched aloft to check on the alignment.

John Toepfer putting the radio harness on a harrier.

Timing was absolutely essential for putting the radios on. Tom Dunstan, an expert on instrumented raptors, offered to come from Illinois to help on the morning of July 17. That meant that we had to catch a *pair* of harriers that very morning. A large order. Frederick is a top-notch trapper so I enlisted his help. By July 17 we had already trapped some of the easily caught, good reactors so to play it safe, two crews—one led by Frederick and the other led by me—set out with owls, to try to catch a pair. My crew and I caught the female only. Frederick and his caught the pair!

In the meantime Dunstan found he couldn't manage to come. So John Toepfer, whose only experience was instrumenting prairie chickens, met us on the Marsh to put the radio backpacks on. Prairie chickens are built rather like prize fighters, whereas harriers are more like tennis players. This created problems so it was about three hours before we were content that the harnesses of the pair were a perfect fit. Imping and processing had gone fast. The young ranged from 2 to 10 days in age, and I worried about the delay created by fitting harnesses. "Let's get those birds back to their kids as quickly as we can."

Finally we released both birds about 30 yards from the nest. Both flew well on release. We celebrated by serving hot coffee.

For the next day and a half, the male spent much more time than usual on the ground . . . apparently getting adjusted to the backpack. We flushed him three times during this period to make sure that he was all right, and hadn't gotten himself entangled in something. Each time he flew well, but not very far.

On the morning of the third day we saw him on a long flight for the first time. His adjustment period appeared to be over. It had lasted 42 hours.

Quoting from a paper that I published with Deann: (31)

The female's radio was highly erratic during the first few days and we could not keep contact with her. She also spent an abnormal amount of time on the ground during the afternoon of the 17th, and during the following morning, but we lost her about 11 a.m. on the 18th. We did not see her in normal hunting flight until the 22nd, the sixth day. Her signal came through a few times during the intervening days, but we know too little about what she was doing to be able to specify the length of her period of adjustment. During the adjustment period the harriers abandoned their young. We were, therefore, no longer dealing with a pair of nesting harriers.

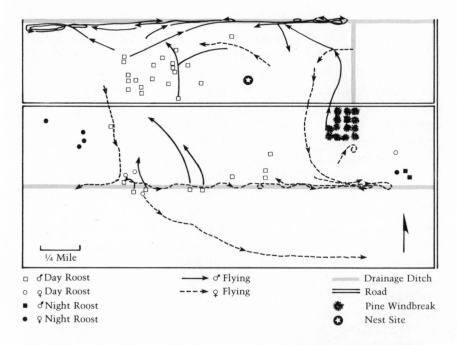

□	♂ Day Roost	⟶	♂ Flying		Drainage Ditch
○	♀ Day Roost	---→	♀ Flying		Road
■	♂ Night Roost			✿	Pine Windbreak
●	♀ Night Roost			✪	Nest Site

The daily cruising range of the harriers covered an area one and one quarter miles by two and three quarter miles. (31) They did not utilize all parts of the area equally. Each bird seemed to have its own favorite hunting grounds, but not all hunting was exclusively within these areas. We saw the female hunting within the male's hunting area only once. The male was flushed four times within the female's hunting area. The harriers did most of their hunting along two drainage ditches one mile apart, the female along the south ditch and the male to the north. Roads and trails simplified triangulation.

Neither bird hunted over pesticide-sprayed fields, but the female hunted within 660 yards of one. Perhaps they'd have hunted over more territory if they had been feeding their young.

I like to know all about whatever creature I do research on, and for some 12 years I'd tried to find their night roosts, by following imped harriers without radios, and succeeded only once. With the aid of the radios we were able to find nine night roosts. On three different nights we found roosts of both male and female birds. Once they roosted two-tenths of a mile apart; once five-tenths, and once one and two-tenths miles apart. Although each bird sometimes returned to a night roosting area, we never found either using exactly the same roost again. Preferred night roost habitat was in open grass-forbs with no more than a scattering of spirea.

We also got some information on day roosts. There was a definite period during the day when both birds stopped flying and went to day roosts. As the male's radio was in much better working condition than the female's, we were able to locate his roosts more often. He usually (16 times) roosted in low brush or tall spirea; the remaining roosts (9) were mostly in grass-forbs. These day roosts tended to be in more open cover than night roosts. Signals from the radio transmitter showed that the male was not totally asleep or inactive on day roosts. There was a fair amount of ground movement; presumably turning around, eating, or preening. The harriers spent more time flying in the morning than in the afternoon.

Our radioed harriers gave us some information, but not really what we were after. It is curious that they didn't leave the study area within 24 hours after deserting, as harriers usually did. There was another curious byproduct. The paper we published caused a chap in California to launch a public attack. J. Richard Hilton accused me of breaking up a nest, letting the young die, and worst of all, "showing no remorse."

He was wrong about the young. As it happens, there were five chicks and one egg in the nest. The oldest chick was only about five days old. We watched anxiously from a distance, but the female failed to come in to feed the chicks. The smallest was only two days old and little hawks need to be brooded at night, so we took them home. The next morning at 5:30 we put the chicks back in the nest. Then we watched for four hours to see if the chicks were being fed; neither adult came, so we gave the chicks some food. When night came, we went to the nest. The chicks had empty crops, so we took them home again. We left the egg in the nest to keep the female interested. The smallest chick died, one mysteriously disappeared, and we reared and released the rest. They got a lot of tender loving care.

16 Rehabilitation of Orphans

Hand-rearing young raptors is very much like bringing up children. For the most part everything goes smoothly, but now and again—at certain critical points—infinite patience is required. For example, it is much quicker to warm up morsels of meat, pry a tiny downy chick's mouth open and shove the meat down its throat, than for *you* to learn how to get the bird to eat by itself. In the wild it would take food from its parent naturally. It is only people—not raptors— who resort to force-feeding.

That little downy chick is programmed to receive food and to swallow it. The cues that the downy expects to make it lift up its little head and open its mouth undoubtedly are many, and some of them may be extremely subtle. Presenting the cues is like pushing the right buttons in the right sequence. Force-feeding is the wrong button, although sometimes—with a very weak chick—it is the only way to save a bird's life. To rear a healthy chick, it must learn to eat. The longer one delays, the more one is apt to get stuck with force-feeding—and an invalid.

Some people are said to have a green thumb with baby birds. My impression is that that green thumb stems from a point of view—namely, think like a bird. A chick that is too cold or wet is in no mood to take food. Food shoved down its throat at this point may be the kiss of death. It can't get warm and cope with food at the same time. People have to figure these things out. A female harrier might offer a chilled chick food, but if it kept refusing food, my hunch is that she'd respond to its distress cheeps and brood it with her nice warm belly instead. I do the next best thing: the chick goes inside my shirt—right next to *my* warm skin.

For most raptors the next cue is easily figured out. Mealtime follows an interruption in being brooded. The parent gets up on her feet to feed the young and this moment is as though a warm blanket were removed. So I put a small blanket—or an old wool sock—over the chick. Then I have a tiny piece of warm meat ready, and when I take the blanket off, the chick's tiny head is apt to wobble upwards; just a touch on the tip of its beak and up opens the mouth. And when that mouth closes—the meat morsel is in it!

Strong chicks nod their heads, struggle, and manage to swallow their meat. Weak chicks may droop their heads as though exhausted. It takes a great deal of self-control not to help a weak chick at this point, but self-control is apt to pay off. On goes the blanket for maybe a minute, then off goes the blanket, up comes the head and down goes the first piece of meat.

This glorious moment must be well prepared for. The next morsel must be ready as soon as the chick wants the second bite of its dinner, and that little head may wobble up very soon indeed.

I watched preparation of morsels at close range when I shared a nest with Chrys, a golden eagle, and have described it in detail in my book *An Eagle to the Sky.* (26)

> First she took each morsel deep into her throat, until it looked as though she had swallowed it, but each time she worked it up again and offered it to the chick, gently brushing the chick's beak and the sides of its head with food. Her efforts were a curious combination of extreme gentleness and ineptitude. She always tilted her head sideways and held the food so tenderly that she often dropped it. Whenever the chick lay quiet, with head down, the eagle egg beside it was taller and Chrys tried to feed the egg, whose top became wet from her attempts. It was almost frightening to see such pure instinct operating.
>
> In spite of my training, it appears I had romantic notions about an eagle's love for its young. Obviously Chrys was stimulated to feed by the sounds of peeps, but she offered food to whatever was moving—sometimes even to the back of the chick's head. If nothing moved, she fed the highest object in the nest, whether the egg or my fingers.

So I learned that gently brushing a chick's beak and head stimulated it to feed and that the meat should be moist. I got each morsel of meat warm and wet by holding it in my mouth.

Some would undoubtedly prefer to have a saucer of warm water nearby to dip the meat into, but as every falconer knows, meat that has reposed in water is less nutritious. Meat held carefully in one's mouth is simply coated with moisture. The female raptor may even be providing the chick with enzymes from her saliva for the first few days—rather like colostrum in mother's milk. I'm not at all sure that I supply the right enzymes, if any, but my orphans tend to thrive.

Every time the chick actually swallows, I whistle. This is a departure from what its own parent would do, but—like anyone bringing up an infant—I am conditioning it to do some things *my* way. After a very few meals, the chick will learn that the food whistle is the dinner bell. One recognized the whistle after it had heard it only seven times.

The food whistle has two purposes. It speeds up feeding; in other words it eliminates dawdling at mealtimes. If the chick doesn't respond to the whistle, I go do something else. One of the main reasons that a raptor fails to respond to the "dinner bell" is that it is about to cough up a pellet. Hawks, and particularly owls, have bad table manners and often swallow items like mice or small birds whole. Hawks can digest most meat, fur, feathers, and bones, but owls hardly digest bones at all. To get rid of these, they cough up pellets in which the bones are buried in matted fur or feathers.

A bird that is about to cough up a pellet is almost never in a mood to eat or hunt. (My great horned owl Ambrose, if I whistled rather persistently, would cough up a pellet on request. He had learned the food whistle when he was less than a day old and it is interesting that this conditioned response affected his digestive system perhaps the way the sight of a bunny would have.)

The second purpose of the whistle is to assure the bird a safe return to the wild. Even after it starts hunting on its own, the whistle is still the dinner bell, and if my young hawk made no kill—perhaps because of bad luck, or bad weather—she will not go to roost supperless. At this stage the bird is *at hack* or being *hacked*.

Hacking certainly has an unpleasant sound, and many people have no notion of what a hack harrier is. Hacking is one of the gentle methods of returning a captive young bird to the wild. The term comes from *hackboard*—namely, a board to which falconers tie meat so that young falcons, now free-flying, can come for a handout whenever they are hungry. If the bird is to be taken up for falconry, it must be caught before it gets too independent and migrates. If it is slated for release I fasten meat on the hackboard daily, or throw chunks of meat in the air for the youngsters to catch. As they grow older it pays to throw the meat quickly, or duck as the hawk comes close.

One year I hacked back three young harriers: two big females and one little male. Competition for food was fierce. Although males develop faster than females and fly sooner, they are smaller and weaker than females of the same age. It was simply pitiful watching the male trying to get a morsel to eat and I couldn't devise a method for giving him an advantage.

I did inadvertently devise such a method for young red-tailed hawks. It is time to tell the story of Aspirin.

One hot day in early summer of 1971 a game warden brought me a young red-tailed hawk—and a story. He had taken the bird from a boy who had been feeding it dog food. The hawk, not surprisingly, got sick on a diet of dog food, so the boy gave it aspirin.

I thanked the warden and promptly named the bird Aspirin. Petite Rouge and Chickie, two female redtails slightly older than Aspirin, were already in my care. Everything went without friction as long as these three birds were unable to fly. Then all hell broke loose. Chickie and Petite Rouge seemed determined to make Aspirin's life miserable at mealtimes.

Aspirin was not only smaller than these formidable chicks, but he was also badly handicapped by the period in his young life when he had subsisted on dog food and aspirin. At this time his growing tail feathers were stunted and weakened by massive fault bars. His tail hung awry and looked like an old duster. He made a sorry sight trying to hold his own against Chickie and Petite Rouge. Aspirin needed a new tail.

I grabbed him, carried him into the house, and cut off all his tail feathers. They were bedraggled and had the dull brownish colors of the immature red-tailed hawk. I looked for matching feathers, but could find none. I did, however, have a complete adult tail with its striking rust red feathers. After about an hour's hard work, I had imped Aspirin with a brand-new tail. Then I let him go and threw a piece of meat onto the lawn. Aspirin was on it like a flash.

He looked over his shoulder. Chickie and Petite Rouge stayed at a respectful distance! From that day forth, Aspirin, with his red

Aspirin, mantling, displays his brand-new tail.

tail, dominated those two big females.

I never did figure out a way to give my young male harrier an edge, but he managed to hold his own well enough, perhaps through his more precocious skill in flying.

17 *Euphoria and Benjamin*

Euphoria earned her name. It was because she was so different from a certain other harrier chick.

Early one summer I took a chick from a nest, partly to teach the gabboons how to become foster parents to harriers, but also to teach them how to learn from chicks. Then I watched both the gabboons and the chick, I hope improving my own skills as a teacher. People seem to want to urge chicks to eat. I watched this going on right by our woodpile and finally suggested, "Don't urge it to eat—tease it a little. Just as it moves its head forward for a bite, you ought to move your hand back."

It worked.

Pleased with myself, I watched the meal get off to a good start with an eager little chick striving for each mouthful.

What I hadn't anticipated was that teasing might be overdone! Some days later the chick had become so aggressive that nobody much enjoyed going outdoors. The chick lurked in the flowerbeds and attacked our bare ankles as we walked past the phlox.

"What shall we name it?" the gabboons asked.

My answer was firm. "We are *not* going to name that chick. It is going back on the marsh to be raised by harriers."

"Don't you want the chick?"

"Not this one. Take it back. Trade it for another—a small one."

The adult harriers accepted this dreadful youngster, and it was replaced by another enchanting downy—a chick that was never to be teased too much, in the hope that it would develop a friendly attitude. It was a female, who soon earned the name of Euphoria. She seemed to spend her time placidly perched on Cloud Nine.

There has often been discussion as to whether or not people can tell if a bird (or a mammal) is happy. The argument seems to run something like this, "They can't tell you so how can you tell?"

I argue, "They're frisky, in good plumage (or pelage), and they weigh about what they're supposed to."

"But they can't tell you!"

"Neither can a little baby."

People not only wonder whether or not a captive bird is happy but they also tend to fear that it isn't getting enough water. They don't seem to grasp that nestlings remain in the nest—do not leave it to take a drink—and may drink nothing other than droplets of rain or dew until they are almost full-grown. Euphoria showed no interest in water until she was 28 days old, at which time almost all her down had disappeared and she was a dark, essentially full-grown bird. At last she stepped into her bath-pan and drank. It was just a week later that she took her first big flights. This is the type of sequence that one cannot work out in the wild because one can't stay close to undisturbed birds pursuing their daily activities.

I continued to take Euphoria in for the night until she was 37 days old. She slept on our sleeping porch, leaving us in peace during the night. At daybreak she stood on my hip.

When she was 36 days old we offered her a one-third-grown lab mouse, by setting it out on the lawn. She seemed to find it less interesting than the corncobs we had tossed her. It moved. At last she stepped on it, pulled off a hind leg, and ate it. Food! She consumed the rest of the lab mouse. Young harriers make a strange growling sound when they first tackle live quarry to feed on it.

Benjamin became a hack harrier more or less through the back door. The rules of the Project are: do not interfere with nature any more than you absolutely have to. If you find a harrier chick that just cannot manage to hatch and is struggling to get out of its shell—leave it be. That's a rule I once broke myself. I watched a chick trying to make it out of its shell and it couldn't. The shell membrane was utterly inflexible and dry, like the parchment that diplomas are inscribed upon. I spat on that arena of life-and-death struggle, and I licked the line along which that struggling chick had pipped until

Euphoria stands on my hip and wakes me up. She stands on one leg and then the other.

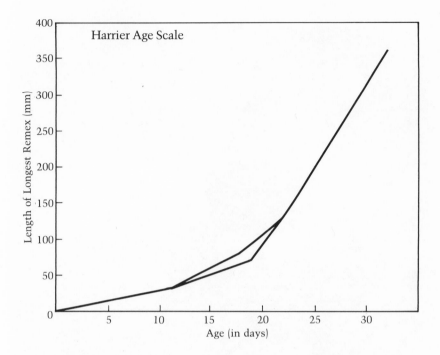

the chick forced back the cap of its egg and emerged successfully. I, myself, broke the rules of the Project and interfered.

When a gabboon named Kevin happened to tell me that the harrier nestlings in one nest were covered with small red ants—and it looked as though the smallest had not the slightest chance of surviving—I broke the rules of the Harrier Project again. I wanted to hand-rear a *male* nestling. Euphoria had been a gorgeous female. I was too busy to take a male nestling from a nest, but egged on by red ants and threats of death, I wanted that chick. I had a perfect right to take any nestling from any nest under permit, but a little dig from the heart sometimes stimulates scientific work.

I said, "Kevin, bring that chick in." So that chick, Benjamin, became part of our establishment.

The next day Kevin said, "The ants were much fewer at the nest. They may have been stirred up by the banding crew."

I didn't listen. I wanted to learn from Benjamin. I didn't say, "I'm glad to hear that. Take Benjamin back."

I couldn't say it. I had learned so much from the witchy-bitchy creature who preceded Euphoria—and from my earlier hack harriers—*I wanted Benjamin*.

Benjamin 25 days old.

Benjamin weighed about five ounces (141 grams to be exact) and his fourth primary was 31 millimeters long. Using the age scale that we had devised, we calculated that he was 12 days old, so his hatch date was July 2.

At 20 days he toddled about 25 feet and he was apt to start home without being called. He seemed to have a stronger sense of "home" than female nestlings.

At 23 days he was up on his legs and running! He also paddled for the first time. Young hawks exercise their wings by paddling before they can fly, and I must say their approach to this daring undertaking is hilariously conservative. They clutch a substantial substrate—the nest edge, or some growing grass—to make certain they will not suddenly find themselves airborne and out of control.

Because I work with young birds I find I get credit for all sorts of marvels. For example people say to me, "Mrs. Hamerstrom, I think it is just *wonderful* how you teach those birds to fly!"

I point out that I can either teach birds to fly, nor fish to swim. They do these things all by themselves; but I can watch their progress and take notes.

Benjamin weighed 360 grams when he was 26 days old. He looked like the prototype of avian adolescence, but four days after this picture was taken he chased a big Lab pup by running at it. The next day he managed to fly three feet to the top of a bushel basket.

On August 4 (age 33 days) Benjamin weighed 369 grams; and two days later he suddenly flew high over the woodshed and into the formal garden. His previous flights had been about nine feet. My notes from August 20 read,

> Until last night Benjy has slept on the porch. I whistle him in every evening. When he is well inside the screen door I throw him a piece of meat and shut the door quickly. Young horned owls call right near our house and barn, so I've brought him in in spite of the fact that he is essentially full grown.
>
> Last night I decided that it's time that he finds suitable roosting places. He may be programmed to learn this during adolescence rather than later, and I don't want to release an inept bird to migrate.
>
> The first night out is always an anxious time with a hawk at hack. If the bird doesn't show up ready for breakfast, one goes to look for the carcass. They almost always are perfectly all right.

Horned owls continue to hoot close to the house and so I still carry him into the house. It is absolutely zany to carry what appears to be a full-grown hawk on a basket-top tray.

Benjamin finds mock quarry.   *He spins to kill it . . .*

Benjamin caused me no worry. This morning I was awakened by the bugling of sandhill cranes. I opened my eyes and there was Benjamin swinging past the north garden. He was flying with a dark bird. Still half asleep, I took it to be a crow. Strange company for a harrier!

About an hour later I woke up again and this time I went to investigate. Benjamin was flying with the dark bird. It was no crow. It was a young female harrier! They looked like brother and sister.

Apparently she has been attracted by Benjamin and possibly hoped to intercept a food drop from his parents. She hardly expected a *person* to come and toss half a rat into the air.

The wild harrier's appearance changed Benjamin's temperament. He had already shown that he considered the vicinity of our house his territory by trying to intimidate that big Lab pup—now the wild bird sat on Benjy's favorite high perch. He dove and smacked her right off it. After both birds put on an air show for about 20 minutes, the wild bird disappeared. I threw Benjy a chunk of pigeon breast. Instead of taking his own sweet time he dove and bound to it as though that big female were right there to grab it from him. Competition has had a most salubrious effect on a number of my hack birds. Benjy was no exception.

August 24:
Tossed Benjy a live but not lively mouse—much as I often toss him sticks to play pounce with. He pounced, started to carry it

. . . and quickly nails it from the opposite direction. Off he goes with his booty.

and then promptly dropped it as soon as he saw it was alive. (I gave the mouse a mercy killing.) This confirms my belief that young do not hunt before migration even more.

August 28:
Young horned owl very close—on weathering yard by back door? Young redtail in field south of pond today. Benjy, at dusk, flew west over woods to young redtail's territory.

August 30:
Benjy leaves. Benjy and black bird flying "in company" S.E. Benjy chasing. Wind S.W. It switched to N.W. later in day. Then a thunderstorm followed by a front—one of the annual patterns that starts thousands of young hawks moving southward —and away!

September 15.
Benjamin has been gone over two weeks. Each day I whistle. Perhaps he will suddenly swing over the marsh and back once more to me. [A young Cooper's hawk returned after an absence of 11 days.] Benjamin left in magnificent condition. I miss him. It is good that he has gone down the wind on migration. It seems silly, but I am about to go outdors and whistle once more—just in case. . . .

18   What the Young Can and Cannot Do

Young harriers are rather mobile the day they hatch. I have no idea what they do while they are still in the egg, but once a chick has broken its eggshell, pulled its way out of the wetness of the inside of the egg, and dried off, it can crawl; it is not totally helpless. If the sun is too hot and its mother is off hunting, it can creep into shade.

One of the most startling instances of this was at a nest where we had set Ambrose, my gentle horned owl, on a perch about three feet from the nest to try to catch the adult harriers. The parent harriers kept diving at Ambrose, but not with enough vehemence to get caught. Time passed. The blazing sun beat down. It beat down on tiny chicks, and I worried.

Ambrose, who never liked the hot sun much, had jumped down off his perch and sat in semi-shade. Much as I wanted to trap those parents, it was time to give up, go in to the nest and take away the set. I walked in to the nest, not much enjoying the intense heat myself. The nest was empty. No young harriers!

And there was something odd about the way Ambrose was sitting. He seemed to be having trouble figuring out where to put his feet. Small wonder. All the young harriers, including the most recently hatched, had escaped the sun by leaving the nest and crawling under my horned owl!

Small young in the nest cannot defend themselves against carrion beetles. Most of what I have learned about small young is from visits to the nest in connection with trapping of adults, or banding

Protesting youngster is carried by its rump and dumped back onto the nest.

the young themselves. (We have not put up observation blinds at harrier nests on the Buena Vista Marsh to watch behavior because I wanted to keep the study standard and unbiased.)

There is a bright orange and black carrion beetle, rather slender in form and 26 millimeters long. I have not been able to identify it, but can vouch that it is an aggressive feaster—not only on carrion, but also on the flesh of tender young living harrier chicks. From my notes July 17, 1962: "6:55 set up at Wheeler nest. 8:15. Caught female (first time she hit net). 3 young OK except orange and black carrion beetle eating middle-sized young alive—(much blood on two young). Took all but the largest young (no blood on him) home for nursing. One died."

I made two mistakes at this nest. I kept the female off too long— from 6:55 to 8:15—so she couldn't pick up the scraps of meat that undoubtedly attracted the carrion beetles. The other mistake was that I didn't clean the nest of these odoriferous scraps myself.

Two- to four-day-old young can crawl a yard or so. Their ability to get back to the nest is something I've been a bit dubious about, so if I see a youngster too far from the nest, I put it back "where it belongs"—like a good parent.

One somehow assumes that if there is no disturbance, all the chicks spend their time sitting within the nest cup. But on July 23, 1960, I walked in to a nest and flushed the female, who had been incubating one egg; all three of her young (the oldest of which was 17 days old) were about six feet away!

Actually it is families like this one that are prone to infant mortality. The egg was probably addled, but if it *had* hatched so late, the chick—ever so much smaller than its sibs—would undoubtedly have been trampled to death. The dead or dying chick might have been eaten by its nest mates, or by insects, or it might simply have been carried off by its mother as a routine part of nest sanitation—like an old piece of meat.

Fratricide occurs in some other raptors. It could occur in the harrier, but all the evidence for this that I have encountered has been circumstantial. (If somebody ever did watch one young harrier killing a nest mate, that somebody could also be seen by the hawks. The chances are that because that person was too close to the nest too long, the young became frantic enough to injure, and then kill.)

Cannibalism is a word that sufficiently stirs the emotions of man that it is hard to find out just what it means. Does it mean killing? Webster's collegiate dictionary (46) neatly ducks the issue by referring to it as "murderous cruelty." Webster's unabridged dictionary (47) comes straight to the point: "the act or habit of eating others of one's own kind." It does not even imply killing.

Not long ago the gabboons gleefully brought in portions of a harrier chick some of which they had extracted from the crops of nest mates, and some were partial remains from the nest. The senior gabboon handed me the remains saying, "Looks as though we'd pinned down cannibalism."

"Yes, but what killed it?"

There was no answer.

Welty (49) mentions that in the barn owl, *Tyto alba,* when larger broods hatched out, "there was a tendency for the youngest birds to die of cannibalism or starvation. Some observers consider this infanticide a wasteful maladaptation. . . ." As with the barn owls, it is apt to be the littlest harrier that fails to make it. It can't

protect itself from being trampled, even if there is no deliberate killing.

It once seemed to me quite remarkable that the littlest one in a brood of five or more harriers ever lives to grow up. When the youngest hatches the oldest is about 11 days old and weighs approximately 10 times as much as that little wet chick, and it must be rather a rowdy nest mate.

There is a mechanism that might have saved its life. I have noticed that partly grown harriers tend to scurry away upon hearing the shrill cries of their smaller nest mates. This mechanism gives the smallest a good chance of survival.

It is interesting to speculate on the intricate behavior patterns in meat-eaters that keep them from killing their own young. The most obvious is the gentleness and care with which the adults walk about on the nest. My best opportunity to watch this was when I was sharing an eyrie with Chrys, my golden eagle. (26) She had more feeling in those great feet than I realized. Once she stepped on a chick's neck, but instantly she arched her toe and did not hurt him.

The persistence with which a female harrier broods her young gives even sickly chicks a chance for survival. One particularly persistent female comes to mind. She flushed as I walked in to a nest. Her chicks lay curiously flat and still. I kneeled down to have a better look, and a not-pleasant odor seemed to permeate the air just above the nest. The chicks were dead, and had been dead for a couple of days.

During the DDT period I came upon another dramatic sight. It was a nest that seemed to be covered with dead birds of various species—mostly blackbirds. I pushed aside this plethora of food and discovered partly decomposed young harriers beneath. It appeared that the dead young had been supplied with food for several days after their demise.

Even extreme displays of parental care cannot help the young if only the male is bringing in the food. It seems that the male harrier—unlike the male red-tailed hawk—is not programmed to tear food for the young. If something happens to the female parent, he will just bring in food and dump it on the nest. It is likely that in the instance just mentioned the female had died or disappeared.

Young harriers learn to catch food in the air—but only food dropped by their parents, not flying birds. Throughout the years, the Harrier Project (especially Alan Beske and Keith Bildstein) has gathered a great deal of evidence that all the food is provided by the adults until the young leave on migration! Their parents do not teach them how to hunt, and they start on their long journey to the wintering quarters with startlingly little experience. Long hours of watching young, both radioed and otherwise, have forced us to reach this conclusion.

Our experiences with hack harriers, especially Euphoria and Benjamin, confirm our field observations, but give little idea of the ways of young harriers after they leave on migration.

19 Hard-earned Success with Telemetry

In 1976 we tried telemetry again. Alan Beske, (6,7) with extraordinary persistence, accomplished three things that would not have been possible without radioed birds. He followed a breeding male and discovered that he had four mates in one summer. This Lothario took up with one female, and as soon as she settled down to incubate, he courted another; gradually he lost interest again and took up with a third; and then a fourth. Thus the polygyny was sequential. It was also unsuccessful—none of the four females brought off any young.

It can be pretty frustrating to spend day after day on the Marsh without being able to account for what one can just get glimpses of. We have noticed mysteriously unbehaved birds. With the help of radios, Beske solved one mystery: a male who abandoned four females after their nests had failed.

He also was able to determine how far the newly fledged harriers flew from the nest and what the purpose of these flights seemed to be. They exercised and played; they went in for mock killing of inanimate objects; and they flew to meet parents returning with food. Their cruising range was about half a mile. They did not hunt on their own.

Young harriers, when they have become strong flyers, can be absolute pests. Some of my hack harriers have harassed me by screaming and dive-bombing (they hit my head, but not very hard), so I wished them gone on migration! We have seen the same sort of unruly behavior in the wild, and one wonders how the parent birds put up with it.

One young harrier even grabbed the adult female by the tail! It has been said about some species of raptors that the adults drive the young away when the time comes for them to leave home. We have suspected this with great horned owls, but have seen no sign of it with harriers. The parent birds that we have watched have been consistently forbearing.

It is interesting that the wild birds and my hack harriers tend to leave at about the same time. Age—about three weeks after flying—rather than parental influence, probably triggers the onset of migration.

Every now and then the triggering doesn't seem to meet the usual schedule. One of Beske's radioed harriers stayed in its natal area for 52 days after fledging. In 1984 two young harriers stayed well beyond what would seem to have been their proper time of departure, and set up temporary home ranges. But these youngsters were different from most. Five of Beske's seven radioed harriers left the study area 21 days after they were first seen flying, and the sixth left on the 33rd day. (6) My hack harriers left about the same time: Euphoria on the 20th day after fledging and Benjamin on the 24th.

Beske, accompanied by another gabboon, Bruce Phillips, actually managed to follow one young harrier as it started out on life's long journey. It spent the first night inappropriately roosting in a dark, spooky pine plantation south of the study area. It hunted over a bare plowed field where anyone would know that there was little chance of finding quarry.

Our banding returns showed that the Buena Vista Marsh harriers tended to head in a southeasterly direction. We erroneously assumed that the young harriers would go straight to their winter quarters—essentially non-stop, like merlins—but no, this one and two others followed less closely, headed for stopover areas, and set up temporary home ranges!

A solid line on a map, following the path of a harrier, gives none of the excitement and exhaustion that such following entails. Days get long. Somehow one must stop for food, but one certainly does not have time to go into a pleasant restaurant. One grabs something quick and nervously rushes back to where one last heard the beeps of that precious radio, mounted like a rucksack on a young bird making its first journey.

I thought our first telephone call might come from Indiana or even Kentucky. It came from about 100 miles away, in Jefferson

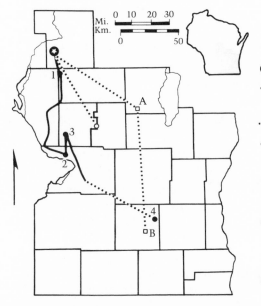

Mi. 0 10 20 30
Km.
0   50

- ✪ Study Area (nests)
- — Known Route Taken by
  Juvenile F2 13–16 August
- •••• Actual Route Not Known
- • Night Roosts of Juvenile F2
  1   13 August
  2   14 August
  3   15 August
  4   16–20 August and Temporary
      Home Range 16–29 August
- ▫ Temporary Home Ranges of
  Juvenile M1
  A   22 August–11 September
  B   26 September–21 October
- ○ General Location of Juvenile F1
  on 22 August

Overall migratory movements and locations of roosts and temporary home ranges of three juveniles August 11–October 21, 1977. (7)

County, Wisconsin. Beske was trying to find his several radioed young, and he had lost contact with one and needed a plane to find it. We said, "Call Tom Meiklejohn at Fond du Lac. He's a member of the flying club and I bet somebody would be willing to take you up." Somebody did.

It was an elderly man in an elderly plane from Palmyra. The instrument panel had a number of roughly cut holes, from some of which gauges and such dangled limply. But the plane had the right sort of struts so that the antennae could be fastened to the wings. The pilot was willing to take Alan up for the price of the gas, which was very generous of him—and very necessary, for funds were short.

Night fell—a beautiful full-moon night. They travelled without running lights. The pilot explained that this was to save the battery since the wind generator wasn't working. They picked up the welcome sound of beeps and followed them toward the city of Milwaukee. From time to time, Alan was asked to check the gas gauge to make sure they still had enough. Checking the gas gauge meant jiggling a battered flashlight into life to read the dial, since the instrument-panel lights were off.

The beeps got stronger near a big Schlitz beer sign deep within the city. Alan memorized that sign's position.

There was gas enough in the tank to get them safely back to Palmyra about midnight.

Alan jumped into his car and headed for Milwaukee and the beer sign, some 70 miles away. He found the beer sign and cruised in its vicinity, surely a strange sight—a VW bus with an antenna protruding from its roof . . . up one street . . . down the next. The police thought so too. Soon there was a squad car ahead of him. And a squad car behind him. And when he turned a corner, there was another. He finally explained his business to the baffled police.

The officers suggested that the bird might be roosting in a city park. Alan knew it wouldn't be, but he went along with this idea to get rid of them. He located beeps coming from an old frame house in a residential area. Perhaps the bird was dead? Being careful not to make too much noise, Alan lifted the lids off the trash cans to peer inside. No bird, and the sound seemed to come from upstairs!

Alan waited outside that frame house in the sleeping city. He waited for the people to get up. Four o'clock, five o'clock, six, seven . . . at last!

He rang the doorbell and the moment that he got into the living room he knew what had happened. There were electronics magazines lying all around the room, on tables, on chairs. A telemetry manufacturer was testing a radio on Alan's wave length, and this had caused Alan to spend one of the most interesting and unproductive nights in his life. So much for the excitement of the early days of telemetry.

Alan asked the man to turn off the radio, and he flew from Milwaukee that morning to a Jefferson County marsh where he located the harrier. It belonged there. His radioed harriers were relatively easy to spot because we had bleached four adjacent flight feathers on each of them. (The bleach used was Lady Clairol "Ultra Blue," which is normally applied to people, in beauty shops. David and Catherine Ellis used this excellent product on eagles. [17])

There are references in the literature to harriers migrating in companies or family parties. Beske's birds did nothing of the sort. Each migrated alone. This was a solid addition to his most interesting findings—the sequential polygyny of a fickle male and the interrupted migration of the young as they dallied in their temporary home ranges on their way south.

20 *Mobbing and Other Trials*

Harriers are persecuted by a multitude of species. The idea that harriers and other hawks have been—and in some places still are—persecuted by man is not a novel one. They are persecuted by mites, by maggots, by lice, and by a variety of birds smaller than they are. For example, "A female harrier hunts along a ditch and a flock of about 75 starlings follows her every turn." In this chapter I shall keep quoting from my notebooks. Harriers are mobbed by sparrows, swallows, redwings and other blackbirds, starlings, sharp-shinned hawks, and kestrels.

They are sometimes mobbed at inconvenient times. A sky-dancing male was mobbed by blackbirds, and a male transferring food to his mate was mobbed by a red-winged blackbird. Is it anthropomorphic to consider this an awkward time to be interrupted? One must remember that food presentation and the sexual urge are closely coordinated in this species.

The little hawks that are far too swift for a harrier to catch in the normal course of events pester harriers. Of 19 encounters with kestrels—and these little falcons weigh ever so much less than harriers—only once was a harrier the aggressor.

Short-eared owls and harriers often share hunting and nesting areas. Of 25 encounters, a harrier attacked a shortear 12 times; a shortear attacked a harrier 7 times; and in 5 encounters, we couldn't tell who picked on whom. Some fights were over food: "They crab; shortear drops mouse; harrier got it." Or, "Shortear chased by brown harrier, finally dropped mouse as harrier closed in. Harrier caught mouse." Owls are more courageous at night, and hawks by day. Although the short-eared owl is remarkably diurnal—especially when feeding its young—it still has an advantage over the harrier in that it can hunt at night. It doesn't compete for food much because it only comes to an area to breed when there are mice a-plenty. (Clark and Ward [15] have an excellent discussion of competition between these two species.) I like to call the short-eared owls gypsies: they move in where the mice are.

Crows and harriers are about the same size. Of 26 encounters harriers appeared to be the aggressors 19 times. Crows eat eggs and they are not above piracy. Here are examples of each threat. A female harrier on her nest was mobbed by crows presumably after her eggs. They flushed her from the nest; when the male came the female returned to the nest. As an example of attempted piracy: a brown harrier carries a vole to a fence post and begins to eat it. A crow rakes her. She moves to a different fence post and resumes eating. This is a small sample, but suggestive.

Our sample size for spring encounters between prairie chickens and harriers is substantial. We have records of 886 encounters during 4,745 blind-mornings assembled over 21 springs. (5) The most common reaction by the prairie chickens was *all flush* (338); next was *some flush* (261); then *no reaction* (102). *Weak reaction, squatting*, etc. made up the rest. Prairie chickens responded differently to male and female harriers. The females, which are larger and stronger, elicited stronger responses. "Using a 4-year sample . . . we found that of 66 *all flush* reactions, only 30.3 percent were to males, while 69.7 percent were to females. On the other hand, of 33 *no reactions*, 93.9 percent were to males while only 6.1 percent were to females."

Prairie chickens react to harriers in various different ways. "Prairie chickens may simply refuse to be intimidated when a harrier comes in—generally so if the harrier is a male, and sometimes so even if it is a female. For example, 'Adult male harrier stoops with outstretched legs at cock—came within three feet of him, but cock stood his ground.'" Another one: "'Harrier landed about 20 feet east of blind. One female prairie chicken flushed . . . other birds remained on booming ground. One . . . cock boomed at hawk from about four feet.'"

Our records indicate only one harrier kill.

On April 26, 1962, at 4:30 A.M., 18 minutes after booming

Cock prairie chicken threatening male harrier.

started, a brown harrier flushed one hen and most of the cocks. Presumably the kill was made then, but we did not discover it until 4:44, when a brown harrier flew low over the booming ground, flushing some of the chickens. She hit the ground about 100 yards south of the booming ground next to an adult female harrier which was plucking a freshly killed prairie chicken cock. The harrier remained on the kill, and, after it had filled its gorge, a redtail, which had been watching from a fence post for at least 6 minutes, flew in, flushing the harrier about 12 feet from its prey. Curiously, the redtail, which one would think capable of ousting a harrier, did not come in sooner but waited until the harrier had filled its gorge.

Inter-reactions with birds larger than harriers usually seem to be attempts to stave off trouble. For example, a harrier carrying prey crabbed with a roughlegged hawk. They both ringed up, and the harrier finally stayed above the roughleg. The harrier does not always win out in such encounters. From F. B. Renn's notes: "An immature harrier catches a vole. A redtail pursues the harrier and forces it to drop its quarry. The redtail settles on the ground with the mouse."

Usually the harrier is the aggressor when the opponent is larger. Of 25 harrier-redtail encounters, the harrier did the attacking or chasing 23 times. Sometimes it was a matter of simple stooping; or, "Female harrier stooping at and crabbing with an immature redtail that was soaring. The redtail was calling like a chick every time it was hit by the harrier. The harrier knocks feathers out of the redtail." Rather rough treatment, but the shoe can be on the other foot. "Checked harrier nest to see if the young had been fed; walked up to immature redtail with full crop. I hand grabbed the redtail about 10 feet from the nest. It had killed all four young in the nest and had eaten one. The female harrier was screaming and stooping" (from Alan Beske's notes).

The six inter-reactions of harriers and sandhill cranes show cranes to be distinctly aware of these hawks which are so much smaller than they are. "Cranes begin hopping and flapping when gray harrier is close (40 feet); brown harrier swoops three times at cranes, who jump and beat wings, male and female harrier stoop 1-2 feet from a crane whose reaction was to duck down. Gray harrier stooped at a crane repeatedly for 2½ hours; crane was too close to nest."

Reactions toward mammalian predators tend to be lively. For example, an adult male dive-bombed to within eighteen inches of a skunk rushing down the road. Foxes also create excitement. From Phil Sorenson's notes on June 11, 1969:

> Observed male harrier (adult) harassing a red fox which had ventured within approximately 50 yards of an active harrier nest. Harrier had been perched on a fence post approximately 150 yards from where above incident occurred. The harrier flew directly from this fence post and made 5 consecutive dives at the fox. No actual contact was made: all 5 dives terminated about 7-10 feet above the fox. All dives were made with up-turned wings (as opposed to outstretched) at a relatively high speed. No attempt was made by the fox to take the offensive; rather, the fox crouched *each* time the harrier swooped by. After the second dive by the harrier, the fox trotted 5-10 steps away from the location of the nest. After the third dive by the harrier, the fox ran at a somewhat faster rate, stopped and again went into a crouch at the harrier's approach, and ran again 10-15 steps before the fifth and final dive by the harrier. The harrier returned to a nearby fence post and cackled for about 30 seconds.

From Jeff Pope's notes on June 16, 1983: "Gray harrier stoops several (20–30) times on 2 red foxes. Gray harrier starts stoop from approximately 20 feet, flies downward toward fox at slight angle. . . . Second fox jumps up on hind legs and tries to snatch gray harrier 3 times, but for the most part the foxes ignored the hawk. Lasted about 15 minutes."

Harriers stoop at deer. Deer would seem to pose no threat, but at least one harrier nest was broken up by a newly established deer run right across the nest.

Of course harriers dive-bomb people near nests. Some bomb more aggressively than others. Frederick still carries faint scars from a female who hit the back of his head in the early 1930s. We are convinced that the female remembered our car, a tan Chevrolet roadster, and that she remembered it for a year. We visited her nest two or three times a day to empty the crops of her young for food-habit studies. She used to come toward the car when it was still a half mile away kekking her "displeasure." The next summer a female harrier came toward our car half a mile from her nest, kekking. When we borrowed Paul Errington's car, a dark sedan, and drove along the same road, she ignored it. I am convinced this is a case of memory.

It is curious what prejudices some people have: they don't like to think that birds have memories. Mammals have long memories. One of my hack harriers chased a big Chesapeake over a half-mile, defending the "natal area." That dog was brought to our house fairly frequently. But from then on it never dared leave the car and had to be dragged into the house by the scruff of the neck.

If memory plays a part in mobbing and harassment, it will take some sophisticated research to sort out which creatures are "inherently harassed" and which respond to remembered experiences.

But I have strayed from the subject of mice.

Harrier flies too close to the nest of sandhill cranes.

21 A Mouse Leaves Its Mark on Mating Systems

Harriers are like the men of Islam. Most of them have one wife, but if they can afford it, more. Wealth for a male harrier has various components, but I have reached the conclusion that over much of its range the meadow vole, *Microtus* spp., can be looked upon either as wealth, or as a most extraordinarily powerful force. Voles regulate how many mates the older males are going to take on, and usually guide whether or not the young males will breed in their first season!

Many people liked to believe that hawks—at least some of them—were the farmer's best friend, and that crops would be demolished by vermin if it weren't for the splendid work performed by hawks and owls in the best interests of man. I'm convinced that this was primarily propaganda to "justify" the existence of raptors, which were indiscriminately shot in the early part of this century. Corpses of harriers, redtails, and peregrine falcons were hung on fences, or nailed to barn doors.

I was once asked after giving a seminar at Oxford, "What effect do the harriers have upon voles?" The question had me floored. I tried to calculate voles per acre during a high, and found this attempt mind-boggling. I considered describing the cut stems mowed by the voles—and the myriads of interlaced runways. How many pounds of mice per acre? At last I gave up any sort of numerical answer. "Harriers probably have about the same effect on voles that a man has on mosquitoes when he's standing outside a cabin and swatting them at dusk."

It is the voles' effect on the harriers that my project has finally firmly documented—by setting mouse traps outdoors: a total of 25,925 Victor breakback mouse traps.

Polygyny occurred most often during vole highs. There was none during the DDT period. Polygyny seems to be on the increase on the Buena Vista Marsh. In 1979, for example, 21 of 34 nests were polygynous: six cases of bigamy and three of "trigamy." Thirty-six of the breeding adults were marked. I would have little confidence in my counts of polygynists throughout the years if we hadn't color-marked so many of the breeding birds.

To understand a population, it is good to see it at a low point and at a high point.

When DDT struck in the 1960s, it first seemed like an inconvenient interruption in my harrier study. Now I see that it gave me a chance to see my birds at a miserably, but interestingly low point. (I waited 19 years to see it at an astonishingly high point.)

In 1968 there were only two nests on the whole marsh. During some of the bad years, 1967–1970, the proportion of male nestlings banded veered from a roughly 50:50 sex ratio to 34 females: 8 males. Our samples were small, but the dearth of males during tough times suggests that fewer males were hatched, or that a goodly number of nestling males may die before banding time. This, in turn, puts more females into the breeding population of the future, and theoretically polygyny could cause the population to recover more quickly when

The mice rule.

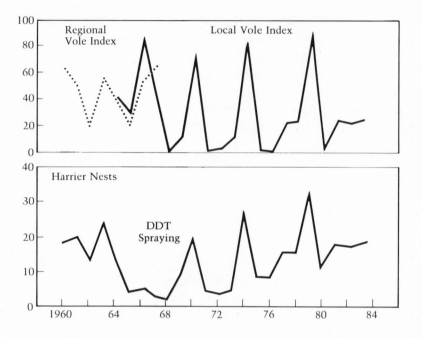

times get better. As there are more females in total, even though they don't do as well individually, they could speed up population recovery. For a fascinating and erudite discussion of sex ratios, read pages 27–31 in *Population Ecology of Raptors* by Ian Newton. (38) (The whole book is worth reading.)

I would like to speculate on the role of polygny. In recent years (19 years after the DDT low) my harrier population has started undergoing a new stress, by no means as violent a stress as DDT, but substantial. It is progressively shrinking range. Agri-industry has invaded the marsh, usurping land which the harriers formerly occupied.

Loss of harrier habitat 1963–1979 was 71 percent, but there were more nests in 1979 than in any other year. (12) The agri-industry invasion has largely—but not entirely—been offset by land purchase and management for prairie chickens. From 1954 through mid-1979 11,377 acres within the Buena Vista Marsh have been privately purchased and leased for prairie chicken management.

Shrinking range plus a vole high may well have crowded the breeding harriers in 1979, and thus triggered polygyny; young males

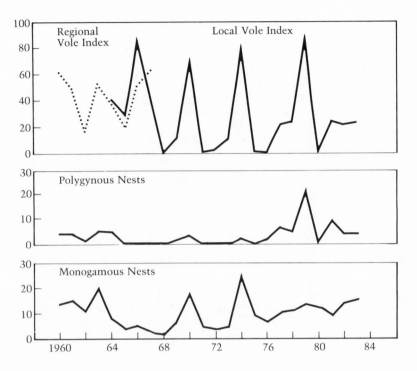

Relationship between vole index and mating systems.

probably got chased out. This time it was a social, rather than a chemical stress. In spite of the largest vole high in the whole study, only one male managed to breed in his first season.

One would expect strife and actual talon-grappling as seen in Idaho, (16) but my harriers have continued to seem tolerant of intruders and merely tend to escort them out of their territories. We keep trying to discover what subtle mechanism keeps the Buena Vista Marsh from being flooded with harriers in good vole years, but we remain baffled. I have a hunch that polygyny regulates against over-population at high population densities because a disproportionate number of polygynous nests fail, but that only accounts for fewer birds in future years. In 1979, in spite of the vole high, there were fewer young than expected.

Getting back to the original question that I asked myself so long ago: Do harriers mate for life? I can well say the answer is no. Fidelity for more than one season was the exception rather than the

rule, in spite of the fact that successful breeders tend to come back to the marsh. In 19 years we color-marked both mates at 70 nests and had only one case of re-mating (12) a case of partial pair fidelity. In 1960 we banded a successful pair; the female was at least three years old. We never saw the male on the marsh in later years. The female returned to the marsh in 1962 and bred successfully with an unbanded male (a bigamist that we caught and banded near his other mate's nest). In 1963 at age 6+ she bred unsuccessfully with an unbanded male whom we failed to catch. In 1964 (age 7+) she re-mated with her bigamist of 1962—a superlative mate, (age 5+) who was now a trigamist and successfully raised young at two of his three nests.

Infidelity seemed to be the rule, and it even seemed that there must be a mechanism *against* fidelity. There was. Returning females moved twice as far from their earlier nests as males did. Charlie Burke (from whose master's thesis I have quoted liberally) measured the distance for 38 returning breeders between current

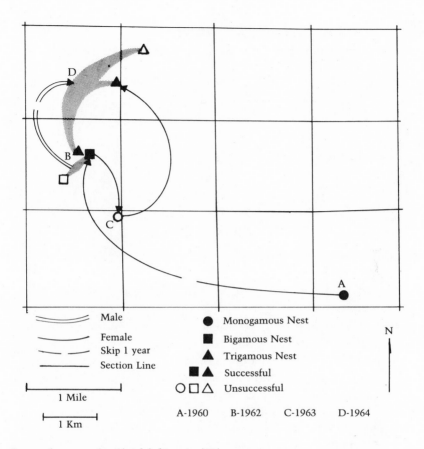

Male
Female
Skip 1 year
Section Line

● Monogamous Nest
■ Bigamous Nest
▲ Trigamous Nest
■▲ Successful
○□△ Unsuccessful

N

1 Mile

1 Km

A-1960   B-1962   C-1963   D-1964

Our only case of a "faithful" pair. (12)

and previous nests. The nests of 20 males averaged 546 meters apart; nests of 18 females averaged 1,092 meters. (12)

It is rather interesting that our one "faithful" pair involved a polygynous male. Having more mates, this male had a better chance of re-mating with one of them. It dawns on one that polygyny probably enhances the chances of re-mating—as close as harriers ever come to true fidelity. Zany, isn't it, that polygyny, which we consider so disgraceful in people, enhances the chances of a semblance of pair fidelity in harriers.

Most game management is inadvertent. The same can be said for
harrier management.

As the United States becomes an older country, we tend more
and more to have stable plant communities; and we tend, too, toward monotypes. There are blocks of forest, blocks of agricultural
land, blocks of suburbs; and most of these blocks remain rather
fixed. But the suburbs keep growing, and we hear more and more
about urban sprawl—an example of inadvertent harrier management. There is an edge to a growing suburb. The former land use—
often farming—has been discontinued. Lots have been staked out.
Weeds and grasses are rampant. Mice multiply. And lo and behold:
in move the harriers and short-eared owls. The benefits, alas, are
very short-term. Ultimately there will be less wildlife habitat.

Some might think it would take a peculiar type of brain to try
to manage two or three square miles of land for weeds and grasses.
Vacant lots are considered unsightly, but roughing-up land and then
letting the plant succession take its course for a few years is a pretty
good recipe for getting mice—and harriers. East of the Mississippi
River, vacant lots if left alone, grow up to bushes and trees which
soon replace the lush, low vole habitat. Further action is needed.

Fire, the axe, and the plow are game management's major tools.
They are also the tools needed for harrier management.

One can raise the question: Aren't there places where harriers
just breed naturally—without management? Let me give some examples. I remember a slough in Iowa where three pairs of harriers

once nested. How many sloughs in the prairie states haven't been drained by now to plant corn?

Those harriers that nested on Martha's Vineyard Island often nested in the shinnery—that vast plain where tiny oak trees grew shin-high. Zealous fire suppression turned the shinnery into forest and caused the heath hen to become extinct; it reduced nesting grounds for harriers, too. (29)

Harriers are endangered in New York State. They used to nest on Staten Island—within the limits of New York City. The last record was in 1961. (43) A building boom, starting in the early '60s apparently ended these nestings forever.

I notice that in most of my examples harriers have disappeared.

They still nest on Long Island near Mayville, in stands of phragmites and poison ivy. Marilyn England, who is making a study of this population, presses through the poison ivy to get to the nests on her study area.

Sometimes I wonder what innovations future managers will use to protect endangered species nesting along the crowded shores of northeastern United States—perhaps some strategic planting of poison ivy?

One of the most fascinating examples of inadvertent, though temporary, harrier management has been the establishment of coniferous plantations in Scotland (mentioned also in the nesting chapter). If you break up a moor by running furrows and tree-planting machines through it, mice will increase. Such machines create excellent vole habitat: they have set back the plant succession.

If, however, you plant trees and they live, the area is doomed as harrier nesting habitat. Patches where trees fail to catch, and rocky outcrops within the plantation, may continue to support a few nesting birds, but the rest is lost. Donald Watson has documented this sad sequence from 1962 through 1975. It looked for a time as though his small harrier population might change its gene pool and swiftly adapt to what he called "forests", but the dark woods, within which his birds tried to nest, are a far cry from harrier habitat. And now his birds are gone.

What I have just described is what Aldo Leopold called a "natural experiment." One can learn from it. If times ever get desperate for the harrier in Scotland—and if conservationists care enough— they could bring in the tree-planting equipment and rough up the moor and *not* plant trees. This might cause much comment, but I

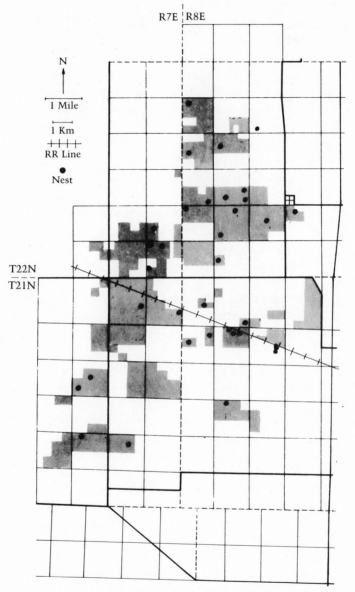

Harrier nests on prairie chicken land, 1979. (12)

predict that such a goldmine of hunting and nesting habitat would attract nesting harriers—if there were still enough left.

To the best of my knowledge, there is no place in the world where harrier management is practiced on purpose, although it might be that somewhere somebody once said, "Don't drain that marsh.

There are some hawks nesting there, and I sort of like them."

The Bear River National Wildlife Refuge in Utah is doing a terrific job of inadvertent harrier management. They maintain older marsh vegetation, which is used for nesting, and they know enough to keep a rotation of vegetation going. The management is mostly for waterfowl, but it certainly is a multi-purpose success.

My study area—the Buena Vista Marsh—happens to have been intensely managed for greater prairie chickens. If it had been managed for harriers during the last 20 years, the results would have been essentially identical. Good prairie chicken management is good harrier management. (27)

Agri-industry invaded my study area during the course of my 25-year study. So did purchases of land for prairie chickens. The loss of habitat ran neck-and-neck with the gains. Of 37 harrier nests found on my entire area between 1970 and 1973, 32 were on lands managed for prairie chickens. (27)

The Franklin Schmidt Prairie Chicken Management Area on the Leola Marsh usually has two or three harrier nests. It is 500 acres of drained marshland and meadow—rich in spirea, goldenrod, and low willow—and almost devoid of trees. It is under management for prairie chickens, so portions of this tract are periodically plowed, burned, grazed, or pastured. (23)

So far I've discussed environmental factors. There may also be a psychological twist. The nests on my study area are inter-related as though the birds were members of communes. I know of no breeding pair isolated from the rest. Would it be worthwhile to manage an acreage so small that only one pair was accommodated? My hunch is that single pairs are more at risk than members of a commune. I have never studied a single pair.

I titled this chapter "Harrier Management." The first step in deliberate management is probably to figure out how to supply a high-quality prey base—mice. First we have to get used to the idea of wanting more mice, and then we have to figure out a way to accomplish this.

Some may have hoped for a cookbook recipe as to how this can *patly* be accomplished. In some ways this world is very young. We are not ready for a recipe. I have presented ideas, and I hope that creative minds will implement them, so that there will never be a spring when the harrier—bright wings flashing against a deep, lead blue sky—no longer dances.

Epilogue

Over the years we have discovered many minutiae and firmly documented the relationship between voles and the number of harrier nests. The next step in learning about harriers would be to find out what triggers this relationship. I see two main possibilities: the trigger may be physiological or psychological. It may be that there is something within the intestinal flora of the vole that acts as an aphrodisiac. I have noticed that the diurnal raptors that I have lived with, tend to eat intestines of small mammals only during the onset of the breeding season—or when they are sick. (It could be that voles are higher-quality food than birds, frogs, and such.)

Falconers use a method called *tid-bitting*. Tid-bitting consists of training a bird to come by giving many little pieces, instead of one big chunk. The bird won't learn much by coming to one big chunk of meat once a day. These many little flights reinforce the bond between the falconer and his bird. When voles are abundant, the male harrier presents the female with food more often than when voles are scarce; when voles are scarce, harriers resort to larger quarry. Thus with abundant voles, the male is tid-bitting the female, which may have a psychological effect on her—an effect that is transmitted to her gonads. After all, if a boy gives a girl a rose a day for twelve days rather than a dozen roses all at once it would surely have a greater impact. Frederick suggests there is the matter of a threshold, and that a big wad of roses might have a greater impact. He is in no position to know.

It would be difficult but not impossible to keep harriers, feed-

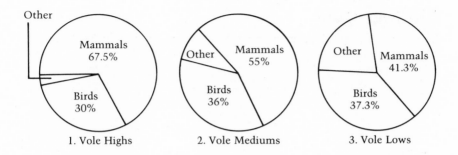

Shift in food habits as voles decrease. See the Appendix for food list.

ing some on voles and others on birds, and see which group attained greater growth of the gonads. It takes skill to keep harriers alive in captivity (one seldom sees them in zoos!). I have watched Professor Leon Cole make incisions in doves, peek at their insides to see what sex they are, and release them. A skilled person can do this in a matter of moments.

I'm always having dreams about what needs to be done next. Another thing that needs to be done next is to trap a young harrier in its winter quarters in the South, attach a radio, and see how this semi-gypsy bird finds a vole high when it's time to breed.

My study should prove useful for monitoring environmental contaminants. So far, pesticides appear to have had no effect on the mouse population. Whenever the relationship between nests and the vole index weakens and becomes disrupted, one can quickly start looking for the trouble. The Buena Vista Marsh has plenty of agriculture, so if some new chemical causes problems, the harriers will probably "notice" it before the people do.

I am saying farewell to this study. I hope the start I made will prove useful.

Bibliography

It seems polite to the reader to make references easy to look up, so each reference is indicated by a number right in the text, and I have often supplied page number as well.

I have kept my bibliography brief and pertinent. For those who wish to delve deeper, or farther afield I recommend:

Glutz von Blotzheim, Urs N., Kurt M. Bauer, and Einhard Bezzel
  1971 *Circus cyaneus* (Linné 1766)—Kornweihe. pp. 337–369 *in* Handbuch der Vögel Mitteleuropas. Band 4. Falconiformes. Akademische Verlagsgesellschaft, Frankfurt am Main. 943 pp.

Cramp, Stanley, chief ed.
  1980 *Circus cyaneus* Hen harrier. pp. 116–126 *in* Handbook of the birds of Europe the Middle East and North America. The birds of the western Palearctic. Vol. II. Hawks to buzzards. Oxford University Press, Oxford, London, and New York. 695 pp.

Bildstein, Keith *in* Ralph S. Palmer, ed.
  1962 Handbook of North American Birds. 3 vols. Yale University Press, New Haven and London.

1 Balfour, E.
  1957 Observations on the breeding biology of the hen harrier in Orkney. Bird Notes. 27(6–7):177–183, 216–224.

2 ———.
  1962 The nest and eggs of the hen harrier in Orkney. Bird Notes. 30(3):69–73.

3 Bent, Arthur Cleveland
  1937 Life histories of North American birds of prey. Part 1. Smithsonian Institution, United States National Museum. Bulletin Number 167. 409 pp. (p. 79)

4 Berger, Daniel D., and Frances Hamerstrom
  1962 Protecting a trapping station from raptor predation. Journal of Wildlife Management. 26(2):203–206.

5 Berger, Daniel D., Frances Hamerstrom, and F. N. Hamerstrom, Jr.
   1963   The effect of raptors on prairie chickens on booming grounds.
          Journal of Wildlife Management. 27(4):778–791.

6 Beske, Alan E.
   1978   Harrier radio-tagging techniques and local and migratory move-
          ments of radio-tagged juvenile harriers. University of Wisconsin-
          Stevens Point. Masters Thesis. 47 pp. (pp. iv–v)

7 ———.
   1982   Local and migratory movements of radio-tagged juvenile harriers.
          Raptor Research. 16(2):39–53.

8 Bildstein, Keith L.
   1979   Behavior of northern harriers on the day of nest abandonment. In-
          land Bird Banding. 51(4):63–65.

9 ———.
   1982   Responses of northern harriers to mobbing passerines. Journal of
          Field Ornithology. 53(1):7–14.

10 Breckenridge, Walter John
   1934   An ecological study of the marsh hawks (Circus hudsonius L) of a
          Minnesota sand plain community. University of Minnesota. Mas-
          ters Thesis. 85 pp. (pp. 30–31)

11 Brehm, Christian Ludwig
   1855   Vollständige Vogelfang. Bernh. Friedr. Voigt., Weimar. 416 pp.
          (pp. 21 and 144)

12 Burke, Charles J.
   1979   Effect of prey and land use on mating systems of harriers. Univer-
          sity of Wisconsin-Stevens Point. Masters Thesis. 46 pp. (pp. iv, 19,
          21, 22, 34)

13 Chesters, G., and G. V. Simsiman
   [1973]   Impact of agricultural use of pesticides on the water quality
            of the Great Lakes. Water Resources Center, University of
            Wisconsin-Madison.

14 Clapp, Roger B., M. Kathleen Klimkiewicz, and John H. Kennard
   1982   Longevity records of North American birds. Journal of Field Orni-
          thology 53(2):81–124.

15 Clark, Richard J., and James G. Ward
   1974   Interspecific competition in two species of open country raptors
          Circus cyaneus and Asio flammeus. Proceedings of the Pennsyl-
          vania Academy of Science. 48:79–87.

16 Craig, T. H., E. H. Craig, and Jeffrey S. Marks
   1982   Aerial talon-grappling in northern harriers. Condor. 84:239.

17 Ellis, David H., and Catherine H. Ellis
   1975   Color marking golden eagles with human hair dyes. Journal of
          Wildlife Management. 39(2):445–447.

18 Forbush, Edward Howe
   1929 Birds of Massachusetts and other New England states. Vol. II. Norwood Press, Norwood, Mass. 461 pp. (p. 102)

19 Gawlik, Dale
   1983 Mouse trap recovered in a harrier nest. Raptor Research. 17(2):62.

20 Hagen, Y.
   1969 Norwegian studies on the reproduction of birds of prey and owls in relation to micro-rodent population fluctuations. Fauna. 22:73–126.

21 Hamerstrom, F. and F.
   1968 Water and the prairie chickens. Wisconsin Academy Review. 15(1): 10–11.

22 ———.
   1971 A method of recording molt. Inland Bird Banding News. 43(4):107–108.

23 Hamerstrom, F. N. Jr., Oswald E. Mattson, and Frances Hamerstrom
   1957 A guide to prairie chicken management. Wisconsin Conservation Department. Technical Wildlife Bulletin Number 15. 128 pp.

24 Hamerstrom, Frances
   1968 Ageing and sexing harriers. Inland Bird Banding News. 40(2):43–46.

25 ———.
   1969 A harrier population study. pp. 367–383 in Hickey, Joseph J., ed. Peregrine falcon populations: their biology and decline. University of Wisconsin Press, Madison, Milwaukee, and London. 596 pp. (pp. 370, 379, 381)

26 ———.
   1970 An eagle to the sky. Iowa State University Press, Ames. 143 pp. (p. 15)

27 ———.
   1974 Raptor management. pp. 5–8 in Frederick N. Hamerstrom, Jr., Byron E. Harrell, and Richard R. Olendorff, eds. Management of raptors. Raptor Research Foundation, Vermillion, S.D. Raptor Research Report Number 2. 146 pp.

28 ———.
   1979 Effect of prey on predator: voles and harriers. Auk. 96(2):370–374.

29 ———.
   1982 Death of a firebird. Defenders. 57(3):37–39.

30 ———.
   1984 Birding with a purpose: of raptors, gabboons, and other creatures. Iowa State University Press, Ames. 130 pp. (pp. 70–73, 82)

31 Hamerstrom, Frances, and Deann De La Ronde Wilde
   1973 Cruising range and roosts of adult harriers. Inland Bird Banding News. 45(4):123–128.

31A Hamerstrom, Frances, Frederick N. Hamerstrom, and Charles J. Burke
    1985 Effect of voles on mating systems in a central Wisconsin popula-
        tion of harriers. Wilson Bulletin 97 (3): 332–346.

32 Hammond, Merrill C., and C. J. Henry
    1949 Success of marsh hawk nests in North Dakota. Auk. 66(3):
        271–274.

33 Harrell, Byron E., ed.
    1974 Proceedings of the conference on raptor conservation techniques,
        Fort Collins, Colorado, 22–24 March 1973. Part 5. Rehabilitation
        and pathology. Raptor Research. 8(1/2):37–44.

34 Hecht, William Robert
    1951 Nesting of the marsh hawk at Delta, Manitoba. Wilson Bulletin.
        63(3):167–176.

35 Hickey, Joseph J., ed.
    1969 Peregrine falcon populations: their biology and decline. University
        of Wisconsin Press, Madison, Milwaukee, and London. 596 pp.

36 Hollom, P. A. D., ed.
    1952 The popular handbook of British birds. H. F. and G. Witherby, Lim-
        ited, London. 424 pp. (pp. 103–106)

37 Libby, J. L., and C. F. Koval
    1970 Wisconsin commercial fruit, vegetable, and processing crop acre-
        age and insecticide use survey 1969. University of Wisconsin/Ex-
        tension, Madison. Resource Report 13.

38 Newton, Ian
    1979 Population ecology of raptors. Buteo Books, Vermillion, S.D. 399
        pp. (pp. 27–31)

39 Peterson, Roger Tory, Guy Montfort, and P. A. D. Hollom
    1954 A field guide to the birds of Britain and Europe. Houghton Mifflin
        Company, Boston. 318 pp. (p. 62)

40 Scharf, William C., and Edward Balfour
    1971 Growth and development of nestling hen harriers. Ibis. 113:
        323–329.

41 Scharf, William C., and Frances Hamerstrom
    1975 A morphological comparison of two harrier populations. Raptor
        Research. 9(1/2):27–32.

42 Schmutz, Josef K., and Sheila M. Schmutz
    1975 Primary molt in *Circus cyaneus* in relation to nest brood events.
        Auk. 92(1):105–110.

43 Siebenheller, Norma
    ,1981 Breeding birds of Staten Island, including Shooter's Island, Prall's
        Island, Hoffman and Swinburne Islands. Staten Island Institute of
        Arts and Sciences. 48 pp.

44 Temme, M.
    1969 Die Kornweihe als Brutvogel und Wintergast auf der Nordseeinsel
        Nordernay. Ornithologische Mitteilungen. 21:3–6.

45 Watson, Donald
   1977 The hen harrier. T. and A. D. Poyser Limited, Berkhamsted, En-
         gland. 307 pp. (pp. 38, 218–219)

46 [Webster, Noah]
   1961 Webster's new collegiate dictionary, *s.v.* "cannibalism." G. and
         C. Merriam Co., Springfield, Mass. 1174 pp.

47 ———.
   1973 Webster's new twentieth century dictionary of the English lan-
         guage unabridged. 2d edition, *s.v.* "cannibalism." World Publish-
         ing Co., Cleveland and New York. 2129 pp.

48 Weis, Henning
   1923 Life of the harrier in Denmark: observations from breeding places
         in West Jutland. G. E. C. Gad, Copenhagen. 80 pp.

49 Welty, Joel Carl
   1963 The life of birds. Alfred A. Knopf, New York. 546 pp. (p. 294)

Appendix

I   **Comparison of Chord vs. Flattened Wing Measurements, and Weights of Adult Breeding Harriers in Orkney and Wisconsin (41)**

	Males			Females		
	No.	Range	(Mean)	No.	Range	(Mean)
Flattened wing (mm)						
Hen harrier	39	334–370	(351.3)	66	376–416	(393.7)
American harrier	12	322–340	(332.3)	36	358–384	(373.1)
Chord (mm)						
Hen harrier	38	325–361	(341.4)	66	361–409	(382.0)
American harrier	14	316–335	(327.0)	39	357–379	(366.6)
Weight (g)						
Hen harrier	44	304–363	(334.0)	61	463–591	(515.8)
American harrier	15	298–372	(367.4)*	42	473–595	(529.9)*

*Immatures were lighter: 13 males averaged 335.4 and 12 females 496.7.

II A Method of Recording Molt

The following is reprinted with permission: (22)

It is high time that ornithologists, banders and wildlife researchers use the same methods of numbering flight feathers. Most professional ornithologists number the primaries starting with number one near the middle of the wing and progressing toward its tip because in most species, the primaries are replaced in this order. Secondary number one is next to primary number one, and numbering proceeds inward toward the body.

Since about 1957 we have used molt cards devised by Cedar Grove Ornithological Station, based on this numbering system. We have found these 3 × 5 cards by far the simplest and most convenient way of recording wing and tail molt, and think they too deserve wider acceptance. As the records are numerical, they can easily be computerized if data become voluminous.

The simplest description of how to fill out a molt card is to give an example (see next page):

The drawing shows a molting harrier on which we were able to determine the age of each feather. (For feathers we are not able to age, we leave that part of the molt card blank.)

Some of the larger species may carry more than two generations of feathers at once so we designate the oldest of these by "V." Wear and fading are the major clues to a feather's age, but can sometimes be deceptive. In any bird the feathers exposed to the weather when the bird is in repose show more signs of wear; this is especially apt to be true of the top tail feather when the bird is roosting and of the wing feathers nearest the body.

It is also easy to miss recently dropped or short incoming feathers, and we *feel* along the row of feather bases to be sure that every feather is accounted for. Many raptors have a gap at about primary number five and care must be taken not to record the gap as a missing feather! Natural gaps may occur among the secondaries as well. As a rule—for raptors—expect to account for ten primaries on each wing and 12 rectrices in the tail. The number of secondaries varies from species to species. Ospreys may have as many as 16.

Molt sometimes makes it possible to sex birds as one or the

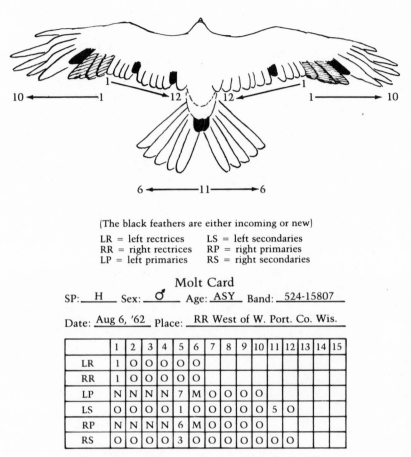

(The black feathers are either incoming or new)

LR = left rectrices	LS = left secondaries
RR = right rectrices	RP = right primaries
LP = left primaries	RS = right secondaries

Molt Card

SP: __H__ Sex: __♂__ Age: __ASY__ Band: __524-15807__

Date: __Aug 6, '62__ Place: __RR West of W. Port. Co. Wis.__

	1	2	3	4	5	6	7	8	9	10	11	12	13	14	15
LR	1	O	O	O	O	O									
RR	1	O	O	O	O	O									
LP	N	N	N	N	7	M	O	O	O	O					
LS	O	O	O	O	1	O	O	O	O	O	5	O			
RP	N	N	N	N	6	M	O	O	O	O					
RS	O	O	O	O	3	O	O	O	O	O	O	O			

Code: O = old, V = older, N = new (completely developed),
6 = 0.6 developed, M = missing

Remarks:

How to fill out a molt card.

other sex may molt earlier; molt often makes it possible to age birds more accurately; and molt is handy for the birds themselves: if they did not shed their old feathers and replace them with new ones from time to time, they would become mighty tattered.

III Residues of Harriers from the Buena Vista Marsh, 1967–1971 [a]

Year and Lab [b]	Sex	Age	Nest Suc.	DDE	DDD	DDT	Dieldrin	PCB	HE [d]	Date	Weight (g)
		Field Data [c]				Residues (ppm)				Biopsy Sample [e]	
BREEDERS											
1967											
WARF	M	Ad	Suc	4.0	1.0	1.2	<0.30			Jul 19	69.4/ 0.0
"	F	Ad	Suc	20.0	2.8	3.8	<0.50			Jul 19	59.3/ 0.0
1968											
WARF	M	Ad	Suc	18.6	2.8	5.6	0.89		1.3	Jul 20	38.5/13.6
"	F[f]	<8	Fail	4.3	1.1	1.8				Jul 28	69.3/24.4
"	F	<3	Suc	3.0	1.1	3.2	<0.65			Jul 21	55.7/24.4
1969											
Bodega	M	Ad	Suc	21.3	0.20	1.15	25.85	1.02		Jun 30	0.0211
"	M	Sub	Suc	15.3	0.28	0.37	0.58	1.74	0.23	Jul 18	0.0112
"	F	Ad	Suc	5.44	0.14	0.62	0.49	1.58		Jul 29	0.0169
"	F	2	Suc	9.67	<0.23	0.40	0.83	<0.80		Jul 6	0.0060
"	F[h]	Sub	Suc	6.13	0.17	0.423	0.595	1.06	0.21	Jul 12	0.0274

III Residues of Harriers from the Buena Vista Marsh, 1967–1971[a] (continued)

Year and Lab[b]	Field Data[c]			Residues (ppm)						Biopsy Sample[e]	
	Sex	Age	Nest Suc.	DDE	DDD	DDT	Dieldrin	PCB	HE[d]	Date	Weight (g)
1970 DNR	M	Ad	Suc	1.76						Jul 27	0.1261
"	M	Ad	Suc[g]	0.49			0.06			Jul 8	0.1190
"	M	Sub	Fail	0.26			0.26			Jul 4	0.1519
"	M[h]	Sub	Suc	11.60			0.47			May 6	0.0702
"	M[h]	Sub	Suc	3.28			0.11			Jul 5	0.1403
"	F[h]	2	Fail	1.73			0.31			May 16	0.1541
"	F	Ad	Suc							Jul 18	0.1557
"	F[h]	Ad	Suc				11.3			Jul 10	0.1832
"	F	2	Fail	0.31			0.30			Jul 4	0.1562
"	F	Sub	Suc	0.56			0.12			Jul 7	0.1109
"	F	Sub	Suc	0.47			2.10			Jul 14	0.1312
"	F	Sub	Suc	0.58						Aug 9	0.1170
Bodega	F[h]	Ad	Suc	6.42	0.19	1.19	0.86	1.02		Apr 20	0.0313
"	F	Sub	Suc	55.7	0.94	2.82	1.82	72.5		Apr 21	0.0285
1971 Bodega	M[h]	Ad	Suc	19.6	0.127	0.68	1.75	4.14		Jul 5	0.0566
"	M[h]	Ad	Suc	27.2	0.11	0.74	2.52	6.49		Aug 1	0.0142
"	M	Ad	Suc	26.9	0.099	0.32	0.698	1.50		Jun 30	0.0637
"	F	2	Fail	12.7	0.136	0.68	3.99	1.28		Jul 15	0.0206

III Residues of Harriers from the Buena Vista Marsh, 1967–1971ᵃ (continued)

Year and Lab[b]	Field Data[c]			Residues (ppm)						Biopsy Sample[e]	
	Sex	Age	Nest Suc.	DDE	DDD	DDT	Dieldrin	PCB	HE[d]	Date	Weight (g)
MIGRANTS											
1967											
WARF	M	Sub		22.0	0.72	1.1	2.1			Jun 6	65.51/2.01
1968											
WARF	M	Ad		0.05	0.04	0.05	0.03			Jun 9	73.9/1.17
1970											
DNR	M	Sub		2.72		0.15				May 6	0.0723
Bodega	M	Sub		8.74	0.16	0.53	2.12	1.56		Apr 24	0.0365
"	M	Sub		1.15	0.076	0.088	0.30	0.97		Apr 25	0.0488
"	M	Sub		11.9	0.16	0.45	0.32	1.91		Apr 29	0.0373
"	M	Sub		1.53	0.11	0.16	0.30	0.96		Apr 29	0.0301
"	F	Ad		57.9	0.13	2.49	0.99	9.45		Apr 18	0.0523
"	F	Sub		2.54	0.076	0.54	0.33	0.81		Apr 19	0.0311
"	F	Sub		4.51	0.13	0.17	0.277	0.38		May 2	0.0867

III Residues of Harriers from the Buena Vista Marsh, 1967–1971 [a] (*continued*)

Year and Lab [b]	Field Data [c]			Residues (ppm)						Biopsy Sample [e]	
	Sex	Age	Nest Suc.	DDE	DDD	DDT	Dieldrin	PCB	HE [d]	Date	Weight (g)
1971											
DNR	M	3		0.57			0.20			Mar 29	0.1595
"	F	Ad		1.06			0.32			Mar 29	0.1432
"	F	Sub		0.13						Mar 29	0.1519
Bodega	M	Ad		4.08	0.16	0.65	0.247	0.55		Apr 7	0.0879
"	M	Sub		0.69	0.045	0.63	0.153	0.80		Apr 4	0.0692
"	F	Ad		11.2	<0.61	5.05	0.32		0.52	Apr 4	0.0986
"	F	Ad		1.88	0.66	2.59	0.186	1.57	0.27	Apr 4	0.0939
"	F	Ad		1.52	0.061	1.10	0.257	1.21		Apr 5	0.0752
"	F	Sub		14.5	0.38	1.44	0.68	1.54		Apr 7	0.0330
"	F	Sub		2.65	0.093	0.121	0.223	2.23		Apr 12	0.0709
"	F	Sub		0.99	0.20	2.13	0.23		0.35	Apr 4	0.1613
"	F	Sub		14.5	0.38	1.44	0.676	1.54		Apr 5	0.0945

III Residues of Harriers from the Buena Vista Marsh, 1967–1971[a] (*continued*)

Year and Lab[b]	Field Data[c]			Residues (ppm)						Biopsy Sample[e]	
	Sex	Age	Nest Suc.	DDE	DDD	DDT	Dieldrin	PCB	HE[d]	Date	Weight (g)

[a] All biopsies are based on breast muscle samples. Two fat samples are excluded as not comparable. Also one 1970 breast muscle sample was so high (338.16 ppm DDE) that I suspected an error and excluded it.

[b] I express thanks to the Wisconsin Alumni Research Foundation, Madison, WI (WARF); Wisconsin Department of Natural Resources, Madison, WI (DNR); and Bodega Marine Laboratory, Bodega Bay, CA (Bodega).

[c] Ages are subadult (Sub), adult (Ad), or in years if exact age was known; nests are successful or failed.

[d] HE = heptachlor epoxide.

[e] Biopsies were weighed from 1969 to 1971. Weight was not recorded 1967–1968, but percent water and percent fat were.

[f] This bird is the Rosenthal female whose story is told in the chapter, The Road to Recovery.

[g] This male was a trigamist. Two of his nests were successful and one failed.

[h] Biopsy residues from the same bird are: Bodega, Jul 12, 1969 and DNR, May 16, 1970; DNR, Jul 10, 1970 and Bodega, Apr 20, 1970; Bodega, Jul 5, 1971 and Bodega, Aug 1, 1971; and DNR, May 6, 1970 and DNR, Jul 5, 1970.

IV Harrier Breeding Performance in Relation to Mating System, 1959–1983 [a]

	Monogamy	Bigamy	Trigamy	Total
No. (%) of all nests	252(76)	54(16)	24(7)	330
No. (%) of nests successful	191(76)	33(61)	17(71)	241(73)
No. of successful nests				
Per female	0.8	0.6	0.7	0.7
Per male	0.8	1.2	2.1	0.8
No. (%) of successful males of each type	191(76)	23(85)	8(100)	222(77)
Young fledged: No. (%)	588(81)	100(14)	38(5)	726
Per female [a]: av.	2.3	1.9	1.6	2.2
Per successful female [a]: av.	3.1	3.0	2.2	3.0
Per male: av.	2.3	3.7	4.7	2.5
Per successful male: av.	3.1	4.3	4.7	3.3

[a] Number fledged ranged 1–5 in all three mating systems. However, five were fledged by 8 percent of monogamous pairs but by only two percent and four percent, respectively, of bigamous and trigamous groups.

V Breeding Performance of Polygynists of Known Age, 1959–1983 [a]

	Bigamy [b]		Trigamy [b]	
	Age of Female (years)		Age of Female (years)	
	Sub-adult	Adult	Sub-adult	Adult
No. of nests	10	25	4	13
No. (%) of nests successful [c]	6(60)	19(76)	2(50)	12(92)
No. young fledged	16	61	3	27
Av. young fledged				
Per female	1.6	2.4	0.7	2.1
Per successful female	2.7	3.2	1.5	2.2
Per successful male	[d]	5.1	[e]	5.5

[a] Fifteen bigamous and seven trigamous nests, accounting for 16 and 8 young, respectively, have been excluded because the females were not aged. Four bigamous nests (7 young) have been excluded because their two males were not aged.

[b] All males were adults.

[c] Successful = fledged at least one young.

[d] No males were known to have had only subadult female mates. The five males with one subadult mate and one adult produced fewer young (17, av. 4.2 per successful male) than the eight with two adults (36, av. 5.1 per successful male). Females of unknown age are not included above.

[e] For only two males (both adult) could all three females (all adult) be aged. Data for unsuccessful females are strongly biassed toward apparent failure because failed nests gave fewer chances to determine the female's age. All menages with unknown females are therefore omitted; three of them did include subadult females.

VI Miscellaneous Notes of Food Items Taken by Harriers, 1964–1983, Arranged Roughly by Size

Vole Years	Mammals	Birds	Other
Low years (vole indexes 14 and under)*	10 meadow mice 3 meadow mice? 4 unident. mice 1 jumping mouse 1 young ground squirrel? 1 young 13-lined ground squirrel 5 13-lined ground squirrels 1 ground squirrel 2 squirrels? 2 small mammals 1 mammal (4 *unident. large mammalian? prey*) ___ 31 items (+4)	2 sparrows 3 savannah sparrows 1 nestling bird 1 small bird 7 birds 3 young meadowlarks 1 bobolink 4 meadowlarks 1 meadowlark? 1 grackle 1 *young prairie chicken* 1 *prairie chicken* 1 *prairie chicken?* 1 *duck* ___ 28 items	insects grasshoppers 5 leopard frogs 5 frogs 1 ribbon snake 2 snakes carrion ___ 16 items
Medium years (vole indexes 15–44)	21 meadow mice 1 unident. mouse 2 13-lined ground squirrels 1 small rodent 3 small mammals 1 unident. mammal 1 *young rabbit* (1 *unident. large mammalian? prey*) ___ 30 items (+1)	1 sparrow 1 small bird 2 passerines 4 birds 1 red-winged blackbird 1 blackbird 2 catbirds 1 starling? 3 meadowlarks 1 *hungarian partridge* 3 *prairie chickens* ___ 20 items	1 insect 1 grasshopper 1 beetle 1 frog 1 snake ___ 5 items

VI   Miscellaneous Notes of Food Items Taken by Harriers, 1964–1983, Arranged Roughly by Size (*continued*)

Vole Years	Mammals	Birds	Other
High years (vole indexes 45 and more)	11 meadow mice 10 unident. mice 3 jumping mice 2 small mammals 1 *big mammal* ___ 27 items	3 sparrows 1 sparrow? 1 passerine 2 birds 2 blackbirds 2 meadowlarks 1 *sora rail?* ___ 12 items	1 frog? ___ 1 item

*The curve shown in the vole indices is derived from the number of voles caught each year, divided by the number of trap nights, multiplied by 1,000. The values range from 0 to 89.

VII Annual Occurrence of Mating Systems, 1959–1983

	Years																									
	59	60	61	62	63	64	65	66	67	68	69	70	71	72	73	74	75	76	77*	78	79	80	81	82	83	Total
Total Number of Nests	7	18	19	13	25	13	4	5	3	2	9	20	5	4	5	27	9	9	16	16	34	12	18	18	19	330
Monogamous Nests	7	14	15	11	20	8	4	5	3	2	7	17	5	4	5	25	9	7	10	11	13	12	9	14	15	252
Bigamous Nests		4	4	2	2	2					2					2		2	6	2	12		6	4	4	54
Trigamous Nests					3	3						3								3	9		3			24

*Four nests, not found, have been included.

VIII Number of Successful Nests per Mating System, 1959–1983

												Years														
	59	60	61	62	63	64	65	66	67	68	69	70	71	72	73	74	75	76	77	78	79	80	81	82	83	Total
Total Number																										
Successful	7	10	9	7	19	10	3	5	3	2	6	14	4	3	3	25	9	5	12	13	25	10	10	14	13	241
Monogamous	7	7	8	6	14	7	3	5	3	2	4	12	4	3	3	23	9	4	9	9	12	10	6	12	9	191
Bigamous		3	1	1	2	1						2						1	3	4	7		4	2	2	33
Trigamous					3	2					2					2					6				2	17

IX Percentage of Nests Successful per Mating System, 1959–1983

												Years														
	59	60	61	62	63	64	65	66	67	68	69	70	71	72	73	74	75	76	77	78	79	80	81	82	83	Av.
All Nests	100	56	47	54	76	77	75	100	100	100	67	70	80	75	60	93	100	56	75	81	74	83	56	78	68	73
Monogamous Nests	100	50	53	55	70	87	75	100	100	100	57	71	80	75	60	92	100	57	90	82	92	83	67	86	60	76
Bigamous Nests		75	25	100	50	50						100						50	58	50	50		50	50	100	61
Trigamous Nests					100	67					67					67					100				33	71

X Minimum Number of Young Fledged* per Mating System, 1959–1983

	Years																									
	59	60	61	62	63	64	65	66	67	68	69	70	71	72	73	74	75	76	77	78	79	80	81	82	83	Total
Total Number Fledged	27	28	32	24	55	28	13	11	7	5	20	39	12	7	7	86	30	16	39	34	71	31	29	44	31	726
Monogamous Fledged	27	20	28	20	42	20	13	11	7	5	13	35	12	7	7	78	30	13	29	27	37	31	15	39	22	588
Bigamous Fledged		8	4	4	7	2					7					8		3	10	2	22		9	5	9	100
Trigamous Fledged					6	6						4								5	12		5			38

*This includes some young banded close to fledging time but not actually followed to fledging.

XI Average Number of Young per Succcessful Nest per Mating System, 1959–1983

													Years													
	59	60	61	62	63	64	65	66	67	68	69	70	71	72	73	74	75	76	77	78	79	80	81	82	83	Av.
All Suc. Nests	3.9	2.8	3.6	3.4	2.9	2.8	4.3	2.2	2.3	2.5	3.3	2.8	3.0	2.3	2.3	3.4	3.3	3.2	3.2	3.4	2.8	3.1	2.9	3.1	2.4	3.0
Monogamous																										
Male or Female	3.9	2.9	3.5	3.3	3.0	2.9	4.3	2.2	2.3	2.5	3.2	2.9	3.0	2.3	2.3	3.4	3.3	3.2	3.2	3.0	3.1	3.1	2.5	3.2	2.4	3.1
Bigamous Female		2.7	4.0	4.0	3.5	2.0					3.5					4.0		3.0	3.3	2.0	3.1		3.0	2.5	2.2	3.0
Bigamous Male		4.0	4.0	4.0	7.0	2.0					7.0					8.0		3.0	5.0	2.0	4.4		4.5	2.5	4.5	4.3
Trigamous Female					2.0	3.0						2.0								1.7	2.0		5.0			2.2
Trigamous Male					6.0	6.0						4.0							5.0	4.0			5.0			4.7

XII Average Number of Young Fledged* by Monogamists and Polygynists, 1959–1983

	Years																									
	59	60	61	62	63	64	65	66	67	68	69	70	71	72	73	74	75	76	77	78	79	80	81	82	83	Av.
Monogamous																										
Male or Female	3.9	1.4	1.9	1.8	2.1	2.5	3.2	2.2	2.3	2.5	1.9	2.1	2.4	1.7	1.4	3.1	3.3	1.9	2.9	2.5	2.8	2.6	1.7	2.8	1.5	2.3
Bigamous Female	2.0	1.0	2.0	3.5	1.0						3.5					4.0		1.5	1.7	1.0	1.8		1.5	1.2	2.2	1.9
Bigamous Male	4.0	2.0	4.0	7.0	2.0					7.0						8.0		3.0	3.3	2.0	3.7		3.0	2.5	4.5	3.7
Trigamous Female					2.0	2.0						1.3							1.7		1.3		1.7			1.6
Trigamous Male					6.0	6.0						4.0								5.0	4.0		5.0			4.7

*This includes some young banded close to fledging time but not actually followed to fledging.

Index